EXTREMISM SEEN AS: AN OBSTACLE

The source of extremism and radical militant belief from the development perspective

Henry Settimba

authorHOUSE®

AuthorHouse™ UK Ltd.
500 Avebury Boulevard
Central Milton Keynes, MK9 2BE
www.authorhouse.co.uk
Phone: 08001974150

First published by AuthorHouse 8/19/2009

ISBN: 978-1-4389-9560-1 (sc)

This book is printed on acid-free paper.

Dedicate to my little friend Paul Kauma

it reminds me of a little boy, Paul Kauma, who died at around 6 years old and was the son of the late David Kauma and the grandson of the spiritual leader and my godfather, Bishop Misaeri Kauma. Something special I remember about Paul was the way he detested violence. May your experience be turned to hope and your hope to the of receiving from the Lord of Hosts the fullness of his salvation 'when he will wipe away tears from all faces and take away from all the earth the reproach of his people'.

Contents

Preface

Writing a book is like building a house: it requires sensitivity to the site of its foundations and a careful selection of the right material. This study came about as a result of trying to come to a rigorous analysis of the causes of violence. It asks a number of questions concerning causal issues in a sociological context. For example, what is the relationship between violence and race? In particular, the book focuses on the historical ideology of colonialism and Western countries' dominance of foreign policies. It is necessary to examine the effects of these policies, first to explain the influences of the beliefs and theories behind them, to consider what they were designed to control and the extent to which they have served to exploit developing countries and exclude other races from development, and to call for developing countries to be able to redress these policies by ending the preoccupation with control. In other words, the book advocates for diversified policies that will allow developing countries to catch up with the rest of the world through the open market and for developed countries to increase their contribution to skills training to enable these countries to develop.

One of the major arguments used in support of the existence of a social, political and economic crisis is to analyse the relationship between ethnocentric theories and foreign policies. Can we understand the lack of development in third world countries as emanating from a social relationship between master and slave? This will be discussed with reference to early forms of violence, primarily as it existed under colonial rule or in the way other races were treated in the ante-bellum American South. There were a number of reasons I was prompted to write this book and one of them is the increase in violence, which is expected to persist and has become a continual crisis in one country after another on the content of Africa. Even as I write, there are flash fights taking place in the Democratic Republic of the Congo by those committed to the use of violence – it has almost become a way of life, not only for business but as a means of grabbing political power, and it is a method that has been in common used by almost all heads of state in the region since independence. They might see this kind of action as right; but when will they see the light?

This is of particular concern when instruments of terror are on the increase globally, and this side of argument builds on the recent rise of youth power in militant violence and choosing to die as martyrs. We need to try to understand what motivates radicalism or extremism and suicide bombers who kill and maim innocent civilians. In order to trace the issues particularly associated with individual decisions to join terrorist groups or freedom fighters in other parts of the world, the evidence is drawn primarily from African local newspapers reporting what happens on the ground, from ordinary people's views and from research in the literature, electronic journals and international newspapers from various news agencies in Europe, the USA and the rest of the world. I have also consulted various academic sources from areas closely related to the current concern about the escalating use of violence and also about questions regarding refugees. The book also features various independent voices concerned with the fear of terrorism, domestic violence, crime and human rights issues.

This book argues that terrorism not only puts pressure on society by creating fear and tension, but also does not provide a lasting solution for international grievances. I also attempt to analyse various claims for why developing countries have failed to develop, the views of human rights groups, and how some politicians in both developed and developing countries have misused their powers to create laws on terrorism that in some cases have contravened human rights. In addition, I examine the central sociological issues concerning what attracts individuals and groups of people to be recruited in order to commit suicide on behalf of others. The intention is not only to cast light on recent developments in the Middle East or the Far East and on the growing economic crisis in Western countries, but also to draw attention to the wider implications of and reasons for the failure of third world countries to examine the historical ideological beliefs that may be impeding their development.

The focus of the book is mainly on three instruments: ethnocentric theories, ideological foreign policies and social economic pressure as a source of violence in many developing nations. The method is to question the vision of developing countries' leaders, unanimously agreed in the Millennium Development Goals. In **The History of Development**, Gilbert Rist provides a complete and powerful overview of what the idea of development has meant throughout history. He traces it from its origins in the Western view of history, through the early stages of the world system, the rise of US hegemony, the supposed triumph of the third world, through to new concerns about the environment and globalization. As Russell Madden neatly puts similar ideas:

In an era in which "values" and "virtues" are often said to be tools of oppression wielded by the power elite of our Westernized civilization or rigid, context-less absolutes imposed by a supernatural god, these concepts deserve a re-examination. In libertarian circles, the two most influential modern writers on these issues are probably the Austrian economist, Ludwig von Mises, and novelist-philosopher Ayn Rand. While their respective works share some similarities, in other ways, they diverge radically from one another. Both approaches lead to different implications for the establishment of a free society (http://home.earthlink.net/~rdmaddenweblocks/value-and-vartues.html).

From the perspective of globalization, the Millennium Development Goals and post-development thinking, Rist and Russell Madden bring the argument completely up to date and highlight the fact that global policies seem to be focused on the commercialization of market lifestyles rather than social justice and on Western values rather than virtues.

John Singer (2000) rightly questions the reach of globalization and notes that speculation about its nature and direction dominates public discourse. What form of international order and hope does globalization offer to developing countries? He says:

Is globalization an economic phenomenon, restructuring the world's economic system from within, as in the view that currently seems prevalent in the field of international political economy? Is it just the old world of power politics writ large, on a global scale? Competition occurs among paradigms to explain this phenomenon and the future shape of our globalized world.

Overall, this gives persuasive support to the argument that globalization has been no more than a collective delusion, which in reality has only resulted in a widening illusion of consumerism, despite the mixture of good and bad information disseminated about its intentions and its outcomes.

Whether or not that is true, situational prevention through lucid and powerful economic market control is a more essential concern than ever for economic practitioners (Rist, XXXX). It is for this reason that the lack of a moral sense in foreign policy is a fundamental concern. What are the normal sentiments associated with soci0economic developments in poor countries in which millions of poor people live? For developed nations who are the determiners of which policies work to ask about the prominence given to the role of economic interests and local development in ethical debates is to debate the moral quandaries involved in globalization. Much of this has generated the perspective of militant violence and encapsulates many of the issues that challenge the ability to find a conscious solution from a civilized standpoint. This increase in violence is the very reason that has led me to decide to revisit a subject that many others have already written about.

This book is a critique of Western countries' foreign policies in relation to developing countries to show how Western interests have created the current violence associated with militant beliefs. I will attempt to critically examine foreign policies from a historical perspective to explain the rise of ethnic conflicts and coups d'état and consider deprivation as the source of conflicts, as well as examining why an increase of radical militant beliefs is associated with a response to the dominance of dictatorship. This kind of analytical criticism has been chosen in an attempt to question the source of the creation of violence in society, to suggest how Western countries can reverse the situation by the use of diversity in foreign policies, and to turn the past into lessons for both developed and developing countries on the potential of democratic rule to reduce the level of violence.

The book therefore concentrates on Western theories and diverse measures originating from the colonial period as well as the present. I do not mention the massive failures of developing countries' leaders, especially the way they misuse foreign aid and natural resources, as thoroughly addressing the dilemmas of foreign policy in developing countries would require a book in itself. I talk partly from personal experience, since early in my 20s I was forced in exile after my father was killed in the political troubles in Uganda. I can therefore contextualize my entire life as a victim attempting to explain a decade of violence. Though it may sound unethical in my case to act like a medical practitioner diagnosing his own lover, nevertheless it would be naive to act like a fly on the wall and not utilize my involvement.

Despite the fact that violence has been part of society for centuries, the recent increase in violence is a demonstration of frustration and it is high time the causes of frustration were addressed. It is important for all countries, developed and developing, and for men, women and children alike to know the dangers of violence. The damage and the trauma that violence causes have a tremendously negative effect on victims, if indeed they survive, and there is a dire need to make developing countries' leaders move away from the use of violence. I believe violence is a problem that starts in one's mind and if people's mentalities are not changed, then it is difficult to eliminate it. The argument of this book is to say 'no to violence'. In this way we can all live in peace and in harmony with one another.

The developed nations cannot simply sit back and watch as millions of innocent people are being killed. There must be an end to the barbaric ideological theories used in discriminatory foreign policies. The level of violence faced by millions of civilians has systemically forced them to become refugees within and outside their countries, as a result of dictatorships created by the use of unwise policies of political dominance by both foreign and local governments.

Let me offer you a powerful example, from a recent report by CNN:

Bedraggled, hungry and dazed, the refugees arrived on the shores of Thailand after fleeing one of the most repressive governments in the world -- the hard-line military regime in Myanmar, also known as Burma. But a CNN investigation has uncovered evidence that for hundreds of Rohingya refugees -- members of a Muslim minority group -- abuse and abandonment at sea were what awaited them in Thailand, at the hands of Thai authorities...

CNN's investigation... -- based on accounts from tourists, sources in Thailand and a Rohingya refugee who said he was on a boat towed back out to sea -- helps to piece together a picture of survival thwarted by an organized effort not just to repel arriving refugees, but to hold them prisoner on shore, drag them in flimsy boats far out to sea and then abandon them (http://edition.cnn.com/2009/WORLD/asiapcf/01/25/thailand.refugees/index).

What this book repeatedly asks is what causes of millions of people in developing countries to become refugees, apparently caught up in human-made catastrophes and struggling for survival. Why are they forced to free their home country following persecution on the grounds of their ethnic origin, culture, religious experience or political beliefs? It argues that repressive and dictatorial regimes dominate their citizens to such an extent that they blur the distinction between violence committed by the regime and that committed by rebellious groups, which leads to an increase in refugees. Just recently a Ugandan rebel group (the Lord's Resistance) has been operating in impenetrable tropical forest covering the border areas between the Democratic Republic of the Congo, Uganda and Sudan. Hundreds of Congolese and Sudanese civilians have been beaten, axed and burned to death in recent months and hundreds more, particularly children and young girls, have been abducted and forcefully recruited into the rebel force to increase its numbers.

Most internally displaced children end up as street children; many refugees are unaccompanied and venerable to abuse by anyone. A great number of children have been orphaned by such conflicts and lost both loved ones and breadwinners. The mourning process has several phrases, the first of which is accepting the loss. Trauma is overwhelming experiences during which, however briefly, we lose all the familiar faculties that help us make sense of the world, such as concentration and the ability to think and control our mind. This "splitting" can be reflected within some individual refugees who lose their sense of self and isolate themselves from others and their feelings, and are thus unable to link up with other members of their own community.

The loss of control is often experienced periodically at irregular intervals after the original trauma, along with occasional flashbacks of the original traumatic events. For refugees who do not even know whether close relatives have died or not, and who do not know whether they will be able to return to their own country, mourning is a complicated process. Sometimes it is better to try to forget than to face up to the pain of loss. For refugees' children, painful losses may be both abstract – of ideas, a culture and a way of life – or concrete – of people and places. Mourning involves a variety of emotions, including sadness and anger. Differences in the way people mourn may lead to difficulties in both leaving others and in making friends.

It is important to be aware that projections of past political ideologies inevitably distort the reality of the present crisis. In fact, colonial rule introduced a repressive culture of violence based on ethnocentric theories of colonization, and since then political regimes have divided and split people, and many families and communities in exile are divided against each other. Peace has rarely existed and political conflicts and the exodus of refugees escaping the violence occasioned by past colonial rule is conceptualized in Western countries' foreign policies and interests. The use of violence and civil wars are seen as part and parcel of the wider and deeper policies of industrial countries towards the prevalent political conflicts in developing countries. These political conflicts involve an increase in and popularization of the use of military and terrorist violence, both aimed at recapturing power. This objective may be pursued by destroying a factory that is making arms, or putting out of action part of the government army, or bombing an airfield so that it cannot be used by government aircraft (http://www. freessay.123.com/essay10847/terrorismdefinitiontypes.html).

The implication of such developments is that every child has to fight for survival in their own land, millions have fled their own countries and been relocated in different places as refugees. This book attempts to explore where and how this started. It dissects mainstream ideological economic theory to present a historical argument for the failure of economic development strategies in Third World countries. Is development theory eurocentric? I assert that Third World development has failed because of the assumption that the Third World needs to be westernized, representing a failure of inappropriate eurocentric economic developmental theories and prescriptions for dysfunctional social structures.

The book therefore briefly explains the theories that have created this crisis and why it only dominates developing nations. I also attempt to build the knowledge of the layperson in order to explain how economic theories have diversified and gained control in developing countries based on the historical ideology in these former colonies, and provide a critical analysis of the social scientific approach to external economic control and political influence in developing countries and the role of foreign policies. Furthermore, the argument analyses how the industrial Western countries' control over markets has prevented developing countries from engage fully in the global economy.

Acknowledgements

Many thanks go particularly to Elizabeth, Peter and Lydia Settimba, who have been a tower of strength during the hard work of creating this book, and for the valuable stimulus they have provided in our discussions. I would also like to thank my colleagues on the team at Seagull Print Ltd for their forbearance and my interruptions during their work. Finally, I am deeply indebted to Sally Lansdell, who has transformed my unstructured manuscript into a piece of polished work. I am quite sure that all of this support has played a great part in the reconstruction of a disturbing and stressful account of how dominance over others has accumulated violence in the world today, and I will always be grateful.

Henry Settimba
14 May 2009

Introduction

This book's main focus is to argue the role of diversity theory in tackling the promotion of violence and the economic problems of developing countries. The discussion will begin in the colonial period, maintaining that economic development in its broadest sense concerns the dominant ideology of colonialism and the economic exclusion from production to which developing countries have been subjected, reducing them to a permanent position as mere consumers. I argue that industrial nations' transformation of the social order was introduced to exploit the potential of less developed countries, leading to a climate of exclusion, social inequality and deprivation, against which liberation groups are likely to rebel, sometimes violently. The economic development policies of these countries were not formed in a vacuum but founded on a culture of violence. As a result, millions of people in many rural areas and remote regions, particularly in war-torn countries, are still struggling to survive and living in dire conditions.

Globalization is not liberating for the poor and consumerism is divisive. Although Western society's developed values are presented as a force of change, they neither champion the equal treatment of humanity nor open up national borders, but rather put pressure on poor countries to compete where they cannot. There is a need to challenge the foreign policies of developed countries, which should not be treated as formulas or rules set in stone, unchangeable and immutable, but are simply theories of human needs that lead to the unjust imposition of exclusion and economic imbalance. The main question is why economies around the globe cannot offer hope and opportunity to all countries and meet the aspiration for a more inclusive and economically diverse formula.

Because of globalization, effects in one country can affect all other countries, and sometimes in unexpected areas. For example, after investigators determined that a pornographic video found in Australia had been produced in Belgium, a number of online child porn rings were revealed, including dangerous offenders who traded and sexually abused children. In one operation more than 170 people around the globe, including at least 61 in the United States, were arrested (Washington. CNN com/htm.13/12/08). Operation Joint Hammer (Operation Koala in Europe) rescued 11 girls in the United States, ages 3 to 13, and dozens more were located in Europe, including several young female victims in Ukraine. The authorities found connections between producers, distributors and customers in nearly 30 countries (Ibid.).

The social structure as perceived by developing countries the design of the economic structure and international laws and policies play a role in how developing countries and their citizens are treated. A significant body of literature that will be examined in this book illustrates the various methods and tools that are arguably still used by the West as strategies to exclude other races from achieving economic sustainability. The lack of 'fair play' on the part of developed countries is argued as likely to prolong the sort of radicalism and marginalization of resistant groups that we have seen over last couple of years.

As a combination of both past and present policies, the social performance and economy of many groups seems to have gone wrong in so many parts of the world. Social and economic changes are increasingly leaving ordinary citizens vulnerable either physically, politically or economically, and the attacks of multiple enemies on society have fuelled worldwide instability.

Violence

One of the main issues the book considers is violence and its causes. Surgeon argues: 'The armed conflicts in the "third" world, to which belongs not only the tropical and subtropical belt across three continents, but also countries in the Balkans, the near east and central Asia, are increasing in number and intensity. Most of these conflicts are "internal" in nature in the sense that they are not wars between neighbouring countries. These conflicts, whether rebellions, civil wars, liberation struggles, succession fights or religious campaigns, have certain characteristics in common: they are driven by poverty (Frances. stewart@queen-elizabeth-house.oxford.ac.uk).

There has been a steady increase in conflicts and an accumulation of refugees and stateless people around the world. This book examines the increase in conflicts in order to gain a better understanding of what it means to live in developing countries, to ask whether or not the policies currently imposed by Western countries have any place in a globalized world, and to question what measures might be taken to overcome the refugee crisis. It will also consider a question posed by Hannah Arendt: How can states guarantee respect for human rights to those whom states do not even recognize to be human? The purpose of this is to assess the effect of democratic rule in developing countries and of policy interest in ideas of disorder and wider sources of conflict in the developmental context in reducing the use of violence.

From a social perspective, violence is consistently identified as a cultural behaviour that initially may start within the family or society but then develops in more widespread ruthless behaviour and abuse. Such behaviour is an obstacle to achieving freedom and democratic rule, particularly actions involving physical force or unlawful intimidation, resulting in loss, injury or constraint for individuals or groups, loss of self-determination and a lack of ability for society to develop in accordance with its national interests.

In this context, the book will explore the shifting boundaries of political and ideological culture and neo-colonial policies, in particular in developing countries. It will examine some of the social consequences of a preoccupation with disorder and civil unrest in terms of drawing developing countries into political conflicts and fermenting an attitude of intolerance in governance. Of course, the problem of inadequate leadership in developing countries is well documented, particularly in connection with dictatorship. Dictatorial leadership affects the efficient use of national resources and retards efforts to respond effectively to changing external environmental factors.

However, the main concern here is to examine foreign policies and theories of the influence and impact of militarism, for example the tensions and foreign policy issues related to the sale of armaments in the context of contemporary political conflicts. The politics of arm sales make it hard for Western countries to practise what they preach in terms of ethics and democratic values. However, looking at this situation critically, it is a real difficulty for industrial countries to find a balance between their view of democratic rule and their role as guarantors of peace on the one hand, and the fact that the continual use of violence is prolonged through the sales of arms on the other, particularly considering that the armaments industry creates employment for their citizens.

Although there seems to be no easy way out, the burden cast by those policies and a refusal to criticize the present state of affairs certainly are not reconcilable with claims to civilization. The use of violence has no value or place in any civilized state and is largely irrelevant to modern society. It serves the dominant theory of a few people who dominate over the majority, but it does demonstrate the development of either democracy or civilization.

Nevertheless, 8 out of 10 of the world's poorest countries are suffering, or have recently suffered, from large-scale violent conflict. Wars in developing countries involve heavy human, economic and social costs and are a major cause of poverty and underdevelopment (Frances.stewart@queen-elizabeth-house.oxford.ac.uk) The extra infant deaths caused by the war in Cambodia, for example, were estimated to be 3% of the country's 1990 population. Most current conflicts, such as in the Sudan or the Congo, are within states, although there is often considerable outside intervention, as in. In the past 30 years Africa has been especially badly affected by war (*Ibid.*)

The appalling violence in developing countries calls for every effort from industrial nations to find an alternative response to bridge the huge gap between those who live in poverty and those who control and dominate the power to create change, in order to reduce violence. If the world continues to stick to the justice–punishment option in wars in which both sides have committed crimes, instead of working towards reconciliation, then the laws of natural justice will take their divinely destined course and the world will remain trapped by the very systems it has decided to pursue (Linda Akullo, New Vision, 22 November 2008).

Human rights and terrorism

The justice systems in many developing countries are yet to be strengthened and many remain without a meaningful and democratic policy towards policing. A poll in New Vision, conducted by the

Steadman Group, was recently released alongside a report on electoral reform to commemorate the 60th anniversary of the Universal Declaration of Human Rights. A total of 1,000 interviewees in Uganda above 18 years old accused the police of being the top violator of human rights by dispersing assemblies with tear gas, denying people the right to associate. After freedom of speech at 77%, the right to life was the next most often suppressed at 76%, education 66%, good health 66%, and a right to help from the government at 25% (New Vision, Uganda, Wednesday 10th December 2008).This book will discuss whether a right to freedom of speech and expression should be defended if it violates another supposed right, such as the right to privacy or not to be offended. It will also endeavour to connect this discussion to the wider debate over the nature of democratic rule in society and to argue that the role of the police is in reinforcing the law. I will look at the culture of police corruption and why police officers in developing countries become corrupted. When one wants to deal with police corruption one has to start from the root cause of the problem, which is that the conditions under which most police forces operate, especially traffic officers, forces them to revert to their instinct for survival of the fittest, which nature provides as a means of reacting to prevailing conditions.

In furtherance of what they see as their human rights, a belief in militant radicalism or fanaticism is recognizable especially among frustrated young people. The phenomenon of radical men and women, who first emerged as suicide bombers ready to die for their cause as martyrs, has evolved into one of the most significant security challenges in recent years. Terrorism has been used against governments, but also by them. It has been employed as part of a campaign by guerrillas with widespread support and by small groups. Terrorism exists in societies where grievances can be expressed freely and in those where free speech is suppressed.

The hitherto abstract and theoretical discourse on human rights has developed substantially since the 1948 Universal Declaration of Human Rights grounded it in international law. Attention will therefore be paid in this books to human rights both in theory and in practice, and to the inter-relationship between the two. Human rights are an important area of social life and underpin many political, legal and moral decisions; as such, they are of crucial importance to our understanding of the broader influences on developing countries' political crises.

However, the question to ask is how effective has the declaration been? And what does the implementation of the idea of human rights in international law mean for the concept of world citizenship? I will try to analyze both historical and contemporary events and political and societal structures to examine the role played by foreign policies, and also how the lack of development has led poor countries to their failure to implement and enforce human rights practice.

Achieving the transformation

This book is a very personal statement. It may not make sense to many in an age that exalts the creation of wealth that a theologian or clergyman can offer any insight into how society can be transformed away from a culture of violence. My aim is to raise the different interpretations of people within those societies to show the effects of the prevalent use of violence and to raise both practical and theoretical questions about the colonial past and the still decolonizing present. It is therefore necessary to explore the background to political events and ideologies in order to demonstrate how diverse fundamental influences led to wider conflict. This will be done through a combination of analysis to tease out the relevant structural variables, such as ethnocentric beliefs and scientific theories.

It is my personal belief that it is high time for the UN to help African people live as people used to live, even if they don't give any financial help. There has been little peace since the Europeans came to Africa. As a citizen of DR Congo has argued, 'most of my relatives were massacred because they mined their gold and the army wanted the gold, so they were killed to take their minerals. We have lost hope and trust in the international community. The UN is just an organization whose existence is to deceive the poor that they're protected (DR Congo citizen in Diaspora in London, 28th November 2008).Unfortunately, even the so-called humanitarian organizations are in many ways not always seen to be committed to the cause of those they claim to serve. It is not surprising that locals refer to these organizations as either spies of Western countries or simply a means of creating employment in the guise of neutral humanitarian support.

I believe that it is morally wrong and negates any claim to civilization if we are still butchering each other in the name of power and development in poor countries. In a concern to consider what is to be done about increasing extremism, I am committed to proposing alternatives to the state-sanctioned application of torture, genocide or death the penalty. I argue that Western countries should reconsider the issues that have pushed many people in developing countries towards radical beliefs and to respond with developmental policies that promote a common ground and a universal policy of diversity within unity.

President George Bush addressed the 45th session of the United Nations General Assembly in a similar vein:

I see a world of open borders, open trade and most importantly, open minds; a world that celebrates the common heritage that belongs to all the world's people, taking pride not just in hometown or homeland but in humanity itself. I see a world touched by a spirit that of the Olympics, based not on competition that's driven by fear but sought out of joy and exhilaration and a true quest for excellence. And I see a world where democracy continues to win new friends and convert old foes and where the Americas — North, Central, and South — can provide a model for the future of all humankind: the world's first completely democratic hemisphere. And I see a world building on the emerging new model of European unity, not just Europe but the whole world and free (Forwarded by John Singer, Carleton University, January 2000).

No matter what our ideological perspective, there is an argument for a focus on equal opportunities for all. I believe that it is a helpful exercise for world leaders to redirect their efforts into resolving the lingering weaknesses of divisive economic policies that have been directed for so long at one-sided self-interest, and for the first time to strive to achieve real change in the wider context of diversity in the contemporary world.

Chapter one

The rise and threat of terrorism worldwide

The purpose of this chapter is to examine issues identified as the main causes of violence in society as a whole and to trace the increasingly militant extremism among young Islamic men and women who live in Western countries. Furthermore, the aim is to assess whether this is due to the influence of religion or wider political influences; to analyse whether fears of terrorism are rational or irrational; and to find out which theory best expresses the nature of the fear of violence from radical groups, if any.

Much of the material for this chapter comes from close observation of what happened in the past under colonial rule and what still happens to black people in the West, contrasted with what occurs in the Middle East and Africa. Electronic sources and desk research are used to track current news and to obtain various voices and personal stories from individuals or groups. For example, CNN reports that some former Guantanamo detainees have returned to terrorist activities. An al-Qaeda video showed militants labelled with their former prisoner numbers. Saeed Shihri, Prisoner No. 372, is believed to have been responsible for an attack on the US embassy in Yemen that killed nearly a dozen people barely a year after he was released from Guantanamo (Cf. ABSTRACT OF RESEARCH PAPER ON "TERRORISM-DEFINITION AND TYPES; http://www.freessay.123.com/essay10847/terrorismdefinitiontypes.html)

Furthermore, this chapter looks at people's experience and wider concern about violence committed in the name of peace or changing the world. It will also attempt to raise the problem of bringing suspects to justice.

In order to advance the argument for Western countries' claims to civilisation, one wonders where the advantages are when all sorts of violence are taking place every second in the houses and fields of impoverished countries, and even in the homes and streets of the most affluent cities. This is what society has created and accepted in the spirit of diversity or globalisation, but it has not granted equal recognition and respect to other patterns of social organisation. The rise of extremism and radical belief can be contrasted with what happens globally and terrorism is traceable in social, political and religious cultures under pressure from globalisation. The chapter will look at several possible aspects of causation, including unemployment and community care, to examine the social and economic pressures in society and the relationships of one to the other.

Response to terrorism in the form of social control

The worldwide concern and fear in the wake of the terrorist attack on the World Trade Center on 11 September 2001 has implications for global social control and the rule of law. This section explores the origin of the fear of terrorist attacks in an urban context, its relevance to industrial countries' wider policies and what goes on worldwide, and asks whether that fear is real or imagined. In particular, it explores both the rationale for tackling the fear of terrorism as a proper object of social development policies and some of its drawbacks, including permitting prejudice, populism and moral panic to drive such policies.

The reason for this to consider some of the dilemmas that terrorism poses historically and, by analysing contemporary global security measures, whether the response was the appropriate one. In particular, confrontations between the major states have receded but intra-regional and religious and ethnic conflicts seem more inflamed than ever. Terrorism may arise from religious motivation, as in Islamic criticism of the USA and also the previous Northern Ireland situation; and it may also be pursued by states against populations (their own or those they have taken over).

There have been worldwide changes in crime prevention measures after the bombing the Twin Towers and several militant suicidal attacks in Europe and East Africa. As ABSTRACT OF RESEARCH PAPER ON "TERRORISM- DEFINITION AND TYPES; says, '[The] September 11 terrorist attacks on [the] USA highlighted the vulnerability of

2

the world's most advance security system to the ingenuity of terrorist menace. The attack has given a new dimension to terrorism. [The] [v]very execution of this terrorist act suggests that terrorism has many forms and it can be executed in variety of ways (Cf. ABSTRACT OF RESEARCH PAPER ON "TERRORISM- DEFINITION AND TYPES*;* http://www. freessay.123.com/essay10847/terrorismdefinitiontypes.html*).* New terrorism laws have also been introduced that included an extension of the time allowed for the interrogation for suspected terrorists.

The fear factor that led to the construction of an international coalition for countering terrorism has won tremendous support on one hand, while on the other hand the follow-up actions and labelling of various groups and organisations as terrorists have caused doubts in many people's minds regarding what terrorism is and the identity of terrorists, as well as a definition of terrorism on which all can agree(http:// www.freessay .123.com/essay10847/terrorismdefinitiontypes.html). The harder the terrorist issue is to quantify, the harder it is to defeat.

Nevertheless, terrorism by its nature is difficult to define. Even the US government cannot agree on one single definition. The old adage that one man's terrorist is another man's freedom fighter is still alive and well (Terrorism Research Center: Definitions 1). Acts of terrorism conjure emotional responses in the victims as well as in the practitioners. Although many people believe that terrorism is evil, arguably it is merely misunderstood because there is no set definition. Terrorists are responsible for most freedom movements, even though they have used violence to get their point across to the public (http:// www.freessay .123.com/essay10847/terrorismdefinitiontypes.html).

New US President Barack Obama has described Pakistan as 'an international challenge of the highest priority'. Similarly, the Indian Defence Minister AK Antony has said that India wants 'actions and results [from Pakistan] more than solidarity from the international community' and called on Pakistan to act decisively to combat terrorism. He commented: 'Even now there are at least 30 terrorist training camps operating on Pakistani soil and New Delhi wants all these terror camps to be dismantled immediately. We welcome the US statement on Pakistan (http://wwww.religiousintellegence.co.uk/ newsID=3687/01/23/09). The world has realised that Pakistan is the epicentre of terror. Now the world must take action against terror breeding from Pakistan. There is no answer in Afghanistan that does not confront the al-Qaeda and Taliban bases along the border, and there will be no lasting peace unless we expand spheres of opportunity for the people of Afghanistan and Pakistan in a detailed analysis of ongoing conflict around the world (http://wwww.religiousintellegence.co.uk/newsID=3687/01/23/09).

Let us consider in more detail the implication of this new attitude and measures that have identified social development pressures and cultural changes as the source of the need for a prevalence of risk prevention measures. Is use of actuarial risk assessment techniques for crime control a threat to civil liberties and human rights or simply a benign tool of social intervention? To start with, in the UK the government turned what criminologists describe as a neoliberal state into one where the state is heavy-handed, with new laws for detention without trial and diversion or incarceration of suspects.

These measures caused a very mixed public response: some supported the measures, while others acted angrily and claimed them as discriminatory. However, the majority saw these measures as the only way to prevent terrorist activities and save them from terrorist violence. Many other European countries have applied new directives in social control: risk assessment, regulation and the extra use of technological devices for surveillance, such as CCTV, new buildings designed to protect communities, especially strategic government buildings, streets and all important places that are regarded as targets for terrorist attacks. Governments in various countries have employed experts in criminology to assess and predict the probability of a terrorist strikes.

One result of the new modes of crime control was that many citizens have become frightened about a sudden attack in a public place. The more real and unpredictable the threat became, the more it created pressure for every institution in society to act, for instance the judicial system underwent several reforms in the UK in order to have the power of control over suspects. As may be expected, all these measures increased the fear of crime and 'ontological insecurity', which was partly due to the media and press creating more awareness of any crime committed at any distance within a short timeframe.

The fear of terrorism and the bloodshed and loss of life that it may lead to make the public rather resilient and determined to continue life as normal. After a terrorist attack in Mumbai a member of the public was heard to say, 'Most of us haven't ever met each other but when you go through something like this, you want a big hug.' (International CNN.com/asia, 27/11/2008)

The police gained extra powers to arrest and detain any suspect, as well as the capacity to repatriate any suspect who might have escaped from prison, wherever they may be. It became the obligation for all police services worldwide to cooperate in the interests of public protection. Nevertheless, these extra powers also created a significant degree of community tension, especially 'stop and search', which led to an increase to the number of young coloured people being stopped by police. This created a controversial atmosphere because of the concern about young people from deprived areas feeling victimised by being suspects all the time.

Other voices of protest came from civil rights groups. The incarceration of suspects was interpreted as an infringement of human rights and also regarded as a miscarriage of justice, since incarceration of innocent suspects and delaying their release was delaying justice. The detention of suspects and the methods used to incarcerate them were described as repressive and discriminatory.

These new measures also caused public concern, especially among the parents and families of young people who interpreted incarceration as illegal and failing to charge people in time as a double punishment of innocent people. Furthermore, the effect of keeping suspects away from the public will be considered later to show how this situation forced young people of all races from deprived areas into being recruited to militant groups.

The evidence from Western countries shows that a different picture is possible: people from all races and countries can enjoy the richness of living in a multicultural society. There is also an undeniable recognition that refugee communities, alongside other immigrant communities, have a vested interest in promoting a strong civil society built on shared notions of good citizenship, social cohesion, religious tolerance and peaceful coexistence (Home Office Report, Working together to prevent extremism, August-October 2005:2).

In analysing current political events, there is evidence of accumulating forces that have led developing societies or large groups to emerge from the collective and to influence individuals rather than the other way round, which is evidently currently in many countries caught up in political conflict. Thus the theory reveals that, despite the fact that one might think something is an individual act, it is a social fact. That suggests at least that the problem of terrorism is global and has less of a connection with local communities. Furthermore, to assess its wider consequences it is necessary to analyse the social order, which increasingly has polarised several developing countries into conflict waged by activists against economic injustices worldwide. In fact the invention and reinvention of developing countries' dominance policies are the object of continual contention and struggle.

Why are young immigrants from all religious faiths in Western countries turning against their communities and the values of democracy to extremist radical activism? There are two opposing theories about the way in which the current wider political issues of extremist activism are understood within immigrant societies. First, in order to understand the source of extremism, special attention has to be paid to metaphors related to the way in which the material world is implicated in the apparent 'globalisation' of economic, social, political, cultural and religious beliefs, which especially influences radicalism among extremist groups that is traceable in the revival of Islamic teaching in the context of the Muslim world.

Secondly, when considering these troubled groups the focus has to be on each country's social issues and political developments in the global context. It can be argued that in a religious interpretation, the extremist's suicidal holy jihad is regarded as martyr's death and a sacrificial act, which demonstrates not only the individual's commitment to a noble cause, but also a regeneration of time and the cosmos. Moreover, history is littered with examples of religious radical activists from all faiths who have responded similarly by sacrificing themselves for their faith. Within the globalisation agenda, it is argued that the response to globalisation is one of the wider issues that seem to distort radical extremist groups' beliefs and conflicts with the Islamic agenda.

In the view of those committed to rebellion, they are waging a war on the oppressors. Their concern is over one country's dominance and boundaries of interference in the internal affairs of another. On the hand, this struggle also highlights a whole series of implications of globalisation sidelining certain groups, therefore falling short of a true global vision. In other words, the root cause of the uprising of activism based on radical beliefs is often interpreted by political authorities in terms of violence rather than in terms of social and political issues worldwide and interference by industrial countries. The relationship between not identifying the root cause and maintaining a misleading interpretation of rebellion against repressive regimes in relation to social and economic factors is pointed out as the failure of globalisation to address the plight of poor countries that no longer possess the industries that used to form their economic heart.

Therefore, concerns about social and economic issues lead to a great deal of negativity about unemployment and powerlessness in developing countries, which can be traced back to historical ideological influences and events that have occurred in the last 50 years. Young people in these circumstances are the source of public alarm and a focus on the themes of violence has turned all sorts of reactions from disempowered societies into liabilities.

If we consider the inherent wider political implications as a factor in the global agenda, actual or explicitly threatened violence is seen as a threat, especially to fundamentalist religious values and the whole mission of globalisation. Globalisation can be seen as the creation of an evil empire, a force aimed at replacing fundamental religious values with an alternative metaphor of complex mobile connections: 'localities, regions, nation-states, environments and cultures are transformed in linear fashion by this all powerful "globalisation" (Dickens et al. (2001:104-4).

The use of the law to control extremism

The consequences of the latest extremist activities have forced worldwide calls for increased reinforcement of law and order rather that trying to look at the root causes of extremism. This identifies the lack of compromise in trying to find the ideal approach to the current political situation. It is not my purpose to argue about issues of credibility and which approach is deemed more relevant However, it is necessary briefly to try to assess the effectiveness of the use of the law as a solution to social problems that impose danger on society. Effectiveness refers to the extent to which administrative and legal procedures have served any useful purpose in resolving fundamentally political and economic grievances or in fact have significantly prepared the ground for recruiting more groups of people to fanatic fundamentalist beliefs.

Despite the apparent widespread assumption that there has been a significant reduction in radical activism, it has decreased to an extent in many cities but developing societal grievances have not been addressed. This makes it even harder to justify the use of such measures; to do so is viewed by those opposed to economic design by the state as avoiding many simultaneous social factors. Law and order as a legal instrument can relay public opinion but is an ineffective policy for containing grievances in certain areas. This argument can even be taken one step further, such that laws used politically can easily be seen as the agents of violence. As we have seen elsewhere, laws such those used in South Africa were a form of state violence against its own citizens. Even strengthening the role of law without the cooperation of a society in which young militants relate to the state as preventing them from being free remains a major concern unless drastic steps are taken to address the perceived injustices.

Therefore, it is argued that in some countries, especially in Europe, extremist radicalism can be managed through the population. Nevertheless, the fact is where there is a lack of social justice, agents of law can only put in force a partial breakdown of the disorder that only society can create and maintain for itself. The remedy for the sense of threat and insecurity causes deprived communities to lose self-respect and a feeling of their in society, as well as their ability to appreciate the meaning of living under a wider global agenda. While more young people continue to be born and grow up in the same conditions, we can predict that the same reasons that have turned many to a focus on the effects of local and wider policies will remain a challenge, with broader implications for generations to come.

Chapter two

The source of discriminatory policies

Ethnocentrism theories

This chapter considers the social and economic system to examine the policies on diversity that were introduced in earlier systems. The historical colonial ideology of ethnocentrism is characterised as the theoretical dimension of the political violence that have repeatedly kept many developing countries in a political crisis. This is the reason there is a need to assess the meaning of racism in a wider political and developmental context to see whether the world trade policies set in 1993 to police the GATT agreements intrinsically and unfairly excluded many developing countries and related to previous colonial policies. I will also try to analyse theories of racism locally and internationally from the perspective of a form of social exclusion, which often involves the dehumanisation of an entire group of people.

It can only be argued that the lack of a fair economy amputated developing countries' development at the knees, a circumstance that is not necessarily another 'story' of what went wrong but rather something that has kept them behind and created their political crises. It this situation, viewed as the results of Western institutions' use of economic rules and theories, that has for so long prevented poor nations from making any tangible progress in development. This is neither a post mortem of a specific country or its political policies, or nor a diatribe against the evils of racism and ethnic ideologies. It does not point the finger of blame at any particular group, but shows that what has been happening in the world in terms of human relations as a whole is disadvantaging developing countries. Nevertheless, this does not suggest that all members of developing countries are disadvantaged. Of course, a few are used as agents to carry out the foreigners' mission and these are politicians who base their rule on foreign ideological policies. They are often criticised in that a typical overt example of structural discrimination today favours their own tribes over the entire population who disagree with their policies.

It appears that the choice of this particular approach is based on two main issues of choice and relevance. It shows how foreign policies have wider repercussions in the developmental context of problems linked to violence and that they cover a massive catchment area. It highlights the worldwide problem of political crises and the increase in violence committed daily, either through discrimination or in the name of religious beliefs, political ideologies, race, colour or ethnicity. Discrimination against minorities affects other minorities, for example immigrants with European descent who move to other countries and have a foreign accent are often treated in the same way as others in their new society. It also affects their children born in other countries. The third generation of coloured children in the West are treated as outsiders and as 'others'; despite the law recognising them as citizens, society retains their status as outsiders.

Alexander argues that informal communities are eventually likely to drift into deviant behaviour. Therefore, the public needs to realise that the way in which these informal communities become easy targets of radical militant activists as itself a process of the way in which the problem of militant activists is inflamed and explained (Alexander, 2000). The influence on people of other faiths of both living in poverty and wider concerns is seen a major force behind their joining militant movements. Others who live in developed countries and lack prospects for the future and are trapped outside the mainstream gain fuel for their feeling of relatively deprivation in relation to what happens worldwide, which is compounded in the most deprived areas. In addition, the argument that poverty has further driving consequences for what goes on a wider scale accelerates into young people rebelling against the Western system by equating themselves with Islamic teaching. This is a telling situation when considering the growing number of black men who experience echoes of frustration about their conditions and react angrily, often through the expression of frustration, especially those who live in the West and relate their own circumstances to wider issues, sees the whole state of affairs as social injustice. This may be a result of what goes on locally in their neighbourhood, for instance the use of discriminatory graffiti, music, attitudes and the behaviour of the system, which discriminates against them either through the police or their lack of employment.

According to Garland, members of this underclass very easily become imprisoned, especially if they are black and from a poor family. It is as if just being poor qualifies you to be in prison (Garland 2000:35). Just to cite one incident, a few months ago a friend of mine was travelling on the underground and was picked up by the police, suspected as being an overstaying immigrant whose visa has expired or an illegal immigrant who has entered without valid documents. This friend tried to explain that he was not an immigrant and protested that he was born in the UK and as a British citizen, but no one took him seriously at the police station. It was not until his family presented the evidence that he was allowed to go. This incident highlights two things: first, that a black person's local accent doesn't count in the same way as it does for those from European countries; secondly, that his colour of skin is easily associated with asylum seekers or illegal immigrants.

Until this incident happened my friend had convinced himself to believe that he was part of the community in which he lived, where he had been born, but he realised when he was called an immigrant overstayer that all along it had been a myth to believe that he was at home. In most cases living under such conditions causes pain, fear and confusion to many younger black people, especially those who are discriminated against in the country where there were born and who have never known any other home. Phil Cohen has observed that racism and nationalism are part of their everyday life (Cohen, 1993).

Problems of race discrimination are rooted in beliefs of biological difference based on superior and inferior races. This is in contrast to the objectives of the Declaration of Human Rights, which emphasises equality of conditions in the provision of a wide range of policies designed to provide equal opportunity. The cause of universal human rights long championed by the United Nations was for the protection of disadvantaged groups. The Declaration of Human Rights was designed to reduce the entrenched inequalities in society, which had come about because of racist beliefs pertaining to certain social groups and their persistent treatment as inferior to people of the white race. Inequality was created directly by discrimination that in its turn could be overt, covert or structural.

Structural discrimination is the most problematic of all. It has been identified as originating from colonial days during the nineteenth and twentieth centuries and advanced by the use of biological theories. Arguably it continues with overt discrimination in foreign policies, despite the fact that the concept of race has no biological validity or generic evidence. The beliefs vary from generation to generation, for example theories about black cultural deficiencies and generic inferiority on the other hand and on the other arguments put forward by the defenders of white supremacy, yet this ignores the fact that the problem lies within the deficiencies of the wider controlling systems of white society. However, the analysis of the metaphors of violence and dominance and the ideological theory of home that is central to the rhetoric of popular racism and nationalism in Europe seems to have occurred on the first arrival of immigrants from the West Indies in the 1940s. According to local sources, it was during this period that European home nationalism was born, which in a way explains the deeper consciousness of immigrants' imagery about having a new home.

Understandably, the police face a dilemma when trying to identify who is who when they are reinforcing the law. However, there is no excuse for their not being extra careful when handling a sensitive issue that in the public's judgement might turn out to be a scandal. The situation calls for reform on a wider scale to allow members of other societies to be handled with care. The public often expresses this as the police in the West needing to stop living in the past. If police training is part of the problem, it then needs to be restructured to encompass modern methods in today's society.

Also dominant in theories of racism is a characterisation of black people as underachievers who will continue to underachieve because of deficiencies within their culture. As early as the nineteenth century the scientist Lombroso constructed a theory of white dominance over black people based on the claim that the latter are born with the traits of criminality and laziness. Cyril Burt also advocated a theory of genetic inferiority in the 1960s, although such theories did not receive as much attention in Europe as they did in the USA.

The famous British human geneticist Cyril Burt and his colleagues, Hermstein, Jensen and Hans Eysenck, all gave scientific credibility to the genetic inferiority theory of black people in respect to intelligence (Reger, Gary, Trinity College, Hartford, Connecticut Newsweek Sept 23, 1991). However, the underpinnings of this theory had an important role to play in dominating policy as a dominant tool to rule black people, prominently reinforced by the European idea of white superiority that was championed in the twentieth century most notably by colonialists and missionaries, relying on empirical theories of discrimination. In the 1960s and 1970s, however, educational institutions were encouraged to believe that racism was not a major issue and that the educational system was devoid of any prejudice.

Assessment of ethnocentric theories

The fundamental purpose of this assessment is to demonstrate that stereotypical notions of race and violence in contemporary society have not developed in a vacuum, but can be traced back through the history of well-planned ideological rule through the use of sophisticated theories of foreign policy, which appears to deny developing countries the opportunity to develop and instead makes them dependent on the West. This is the mechanism by which the poorest countries and the poorest citizens of those countries are kept in poverty (Wande Mansell, Belinda Meteyard and Alan Thomson, 1995:119). As Mansell et al. (1995) argue: 'When [in] 1990 the World Bank reported that 1989 was the 7th successive year in which the net flow of money was from the so called developing nations to the developed (ie there was a transfer of wealth from the poor countries to the rich) it probably came as no surprise. What one might have been surprised by however was that the indebtedness of the poorer countries actually increased substantially over those seven years.'

This historical journey aims to draw out the similarities in the conceptual images of race and political violence in both historical and contemporary times. The ideological theories that systematically reinforce the impact of the belief in racial superiority, through various means such as education, provision of loans and development grants used to purchase arms, keep developing countries as clients of a violent political system and maintain the violent rule of dictatorships.

The ideology of supremacy places the emphasis on developing nations' encounters with beliefs and theories of superiority, with the objective of providing evidence of continuing theoretical and empirical accounts of the relationship between race, dominance, violence and dictatorship, particularly in relation to the disproportionate political instability of developing countries and the contexts in which race-related urban disorders in the West have occurred following post-war black and Asian immigration into Western society. The belief in radicalism among young Muslims provides a narrative of such incidents to assess the opposing theoretical accounts offered by different schools of thoughts to explain the causes of race-related radicalism and liberation movements (Keith, M., (1993) Race, Riots and Policing. London: UCL.).

For example, Ziauddin Sardar's explanation of the long history of violence behind Hazbut-Tahrir argues that these groups seek a great Islamic state ruled by a single caliph who would apply Islam completely to all Islamic lands and eventually bring the whole world under Islamic rule. What would be applied 'completely' is Islamic Sharia law. Perhaps the most cogent reason why the religious scholars who first developed Islam's legal reasoning rejected an all-powerful unitary caliphate was that they accepted diversity (Ziauddin Sardar www.newstatesman. com/200511140010).

Interpretations of racial theories and political policies vary across social contexts. The same theories that were introduced in historical colonialism and were based on colonial superiority to rule those of different racial traits, McCullum describes in the conflict in Rwanda as the discriminative theory of dominance of coloureds, as follows: 'The past discriminative theories of the early colonisers in the 18th century persuaded them that physical appearances – Tutsis [were] tall and slim with straight noses and long fingers ('more like us'), Hutus, on the other hand, were more 'Bantu' in appearance, shorter, with broad noses and stubby fingers – were an indicator of intelligence and ability (Ibid.).

Prunier observed that the struggle for cultural dominance and subjugation among the Hutus and Tutsis, the central players in the recent massacres, was exploited by racially obsessed Europeans (Cf. Prunier, Gerard. 1995: 130-31). In fact, from 1930 up to the 1940s, some church missionaries were also involved in promoting the superiority theory where they taught mainly Tutsis, claiming that they were the only ones with the ability to learn (Interviews, Kigali and Butare, July 1998). However, more recently the concept of race has been discounted as having no biological validity and genetic analysis has shown that some 'coloureds' share more of their genes with whites than either do with members of their own race (Gary, Reger, Trinity College, Hartford, Connecticut, (Newsweek Sept 23, 1991).

In order to consider IQ testing further, two points need to be highlighted: the fact that the tests used black and white dolls; and the psychological trauma of black children who were told that to be black is to be retarded. It was a torturing experience to be reminded as a child of the colour of your skin, and moreover by a white researcher. The majority of children identified with the black doll. Though it is arguable that the basis of the IQ testing was reasonably obvious and clear, the implications of it are crucial. In further tests in 1968 Greenwald and Oppenheim used black and white dolls and asked children to identify themselves by picking out the doll they most resembled; 15% of the black children tested misidentified their black colour. Carrying out tests of IQ by using objects that reflected colour was a reflection of the understanding that the colour black contained the meaning of being black. Therefore, testing subjected black children to psychological torture, suggesting that teachers had stereotypical expectations and in general racist frames of reference about the cause of underachievement. This attitude reappears now and again when white researchers study other races, for instance anthropologists who went to Africa with a set of attitudes and beliefs towards people of African descent in terms of Nubians' understanding of their society.

Often what appears in the scientific inquires are preconceived beliefs and meanings imposed on other people, which to the researcher might seem obvious but to the people tested have undertones that may be meaningless or harmful. It can be argued that IQ testing overlooked the hidden meanings of how children interpreted the colours to respond in the way they did. The mothers of the black children tested confirmed that some of the boys had some ambivalence or uncertainty, noting that they wanted to be white and displaying feelings of distress about their blackness. Even though it would be ridiculous to assume that low self-esteem is a characteristic experienced only by black people, it can be assumed that the dehumanisation process experienced by a large section of the black race in everyday life has a profound impact on their conceptualisation of the world in relation to themselves, leading to self-hatred and rejection of their colour.

Late in the 1960s educational psychologists discounted the earlier findings, apart from the factors of social deprivation and other environmental variables (Ausubel 1964, Bloom et al 1965, Deutech et al 1967, Hunt 1967). The perceived motivation of learning theory, of course, has always regarded the environment as the prime determinant of ability and as conducive to concentration and success, which involves the entire system of education. Knowledge of the setting of another culture and language cannot be used as a means of testing a child from another kind of education system. What genetic theorists appear to have continually ignored is the fact that testing a child from another cultural heritage on Western cultural objects is totally out of order and the highest kind of discrimination.

The earlier work of Swiss psychologist Jean Piaget on a child's interaction with stimulating aspects of the environment formed the basis on which supporters of this theory founded their argument. In applying Piaget's theory, psychologists diagnosed black children as suffering from insufficient structural intellect or from cognitive defects, arising from insufficient age-appropriate stimulation. The notion of black genetic deficiency on which the results of the IQ test depended is without support in the context of the evidence and is more due to the politics of the time, which had made most young black people hate their colour due to their daily experience of being rejected by mainstream society and their segregation in American schools in the 1960s.

Research studies conducted by Milner in 1975 and Lomax in 1977 in the UK tested children African Caribbean, Asian and English backgrounds and revealed a degree of white orientation in coloured British children on a similar level as that shown in the American studies. However, the British studies also demonstrated that girls of African Caribbean background had considerably higher self-esteem than their white peers, and Hill concluded that black girls born in Africa and the Caribbean had higher self-esteem than black girls born in Britain (Milner, 1975, Lomax 1977, Simmons 1978). A study by

Bagley and Coard (1975) indicated that children of African Caribbean background had a disappointingly low knowledge of their cultural heritage and a substantial number of the same children also disliked their ethnic cultural identity. Therefore, based on these findings, racism has the power of *socially transmitted* influence to other races, for example fostering a subculture of racism among coloured Asians and Arabs against Afro-Caribbeans, which is another form of discrimination based on colour of skin or race traits.

This finding confirmed the discrimination by the education system of black children, and that in one way or another successive governments have failed to address the reasons for black children being low achievers academically. It is argued in black communities that rather than assisting black children in schools to succeed in their academic performance, instead they were simply channelled into music and sports, activities at which they were good. The evidence of this is partly the reason that the second generation of black immigrants in Western countries was significantly represented in sports and music. Black immigrant parents wondered why their children were able to perform academically well in Africa or the West Indies, but not in Western society where one would have expected better performance given its greater degree of development and better facilities.

The research findings reveal that racism was deeply entrenched in every societal system, including education, which discounted the belief that education was simply an academic discipline free from a political agenda.

A comparative look at how far transitions in colonial political, social and economic policies and practice before and after the twentieth century are the product of discriminatory theory also sees such theory as embedded in their development, reflected in developing countries' societal structure and conceptualised, contextualised and used to control developing countries. Such theory even lies at the heart of Western countries' policies of abandoning the development of their former colonies. The influence of theories of discrimination not only limits development but determines who would be accepted as the right leader in former colonies and conditions the acceptance of the use of force as an appropriate method of overcoming resistance to change. They have, rather, become part of the dominant culture, a culture historically dependent, for its existence, on the control of these countries.

In particular, to maintain a political ideology that continues in a notion of white dominance dating from colonialism, social control needs to be geared towards serving alien economic and political interests. Therefore, drawing on these influences accumulates conflicting interests from several groups, which can be argued to be the result of a long-planned overarching discrimination and dominant power structure for the benefit of one racial group. The general notion of white superiority encompasses two main issues, 'control and power'. Beliefs vary from one area to another and demonstrate how the theory of racism is embedded in several spheres of social exclusion, political identity and the power to dominate other races in aspects of their development.

The definition of racial policies

Racism is normally defined as a function of prejudice or power. This theory see one race as dominant in the context of the wider system in which it has become institutionalised in the social structures existing within education, trade and politics. Prejudice can be defined as an unfavourable opinion or feeling formed beforehand or without knowledge, thought or reason, often unconscious and on the grounds of race, colour, and nationality, ethnic or national origins. Power is the ability to make things happen or prevent them from happening. The theory is that racism creates the power and the ability to put into effect one's prejudice to the detriment of particular groups. Racism is thus a set of attitudes and behaviour towards people of another race.

Symptoms of racism are a culture of violence and ethnocentric theories locally or internationally that have no boundaries in terms of age or sex. Often feelings of discrimination ironically make people victims of ongoing abuse in international legal jurisdictions. Museminali has emphasised that this must stop if anyone is to dare to speak of an equal and strong partnership for development between developed and developing countries: 'No country must be forced to divert their agenda and resources for development to address this injustice!' (The Times, Rwanda, 3rd December 2008) In fact, it is through these inconsistencies and diplomatic differentiations that one can recognise how internationally developed governments use discriminatory ideological policies to dominate and subject other countries to wars and political conflict.

This will not go away as the source of grievances if the international community ignores it. It is evident that talking about peace without a change from those who cause the violence is not easy. At the same time, industrial countries insisting on the means of violence is not a solution to bring peace in the world. The tragedy, if the war persists, it that it is always the most vulnerable, such as the elderly, the physically and mentally disabled, women and children, who suffer. The involvement of industrialised countries that is now and then voiced in countries caught up in conflict as a result of Western double standards and racism does not only threaten human coexistence, but will continue to divide humanity.

Racism in white society neatly developed into a theory embedded in the belief that the white race was created to rule others. What is not often brought to the surface is how both the victims and the perpetrators of these ideas and acts indirectly or directly cause suffering even to their own people. This is why I argue that racism or prejudice is like a disease, in that it can affect everyone. Once one member of the human race is infected this affects every other member because racism has no boundaries.

Ironically, too often racist explanations push violence onto black people and blame the source of that violence on the nature of underachievement in poor countries or suggest leaving it to them to sort out their own mess. This suggests a lack of understanding that such views originate from a racist perspective. In Europe this kind of thinking appeared in the nineteenth century, where it was predominantly used in the context of a colonial culture of violence and ethnocentric theories to mistreat colonised people and during the slave trade. It is still an all-too common practice and takes a number of forms. It is a mistake to assume that slavery is no longer an issue that needs to concern activists or that people in general do not still feel prejudice and discrimination in different ways. One of those ways is through ideological foreign policies that influence what happens in the government of developing countries. This has kept the continent of Africa continent in a slave state of poverty and dependent on decisions made somewhere else to determine its very survival and existence.

Kevin Bales' documentary on the modern slave economy neatly exposes past policies and indicates that the best response must be linked to a good understanding on the part of development policy makers that society is dynamic and of when development policies favour development (Ibid). If the black slavery in the American South was characterised by high investment and long-term relationships between 'master' and slave, the new slavery appears to be characterised by just the opposite. For 300 years a large section of the human race have been subjected to the rule of ideological racist policies that were embedded in the earlier slave trade. Colonial capitalist development structures in developing countries are a pertinent influence in sales of military weapons and in grants and financial aid. There are also some dubious so-called humanitarian organisations helping developing countries that are only after those countries' natural resources or raw materials, but that are not allowed to trade in the open market without being subject to external controls.

The objective of such policies has long been aimed at racial exclusion, and is one form of disengaging coloured nations from the means of self-determination, often involving the domination and control of an entire group of people. Institutionalised racism has taken many forms: legal segregation in the American South, apartheid in South Africa and, in its most extreme form, the terrifying history of political conflict and so-called ethnic cleansing in Germany (Cfr. Bales, Kevin (1999) Disposable People: New Slavery in the Global Economy Berkeley: University of California Press, chapter one). If developing countries are allowed to develop themselves without this leading to political conflicts, it is argued that with peace and stability on their side they would eventually learn by experience, rather than dependence on handouts. Incoming humanitarian aid raises the morale of the suffering people but never solves the fundamental causes of civil wars.

The type of education prevalent in developing countries means that they still lack the practical skills appropriate to developing their own industries. Therefore, successfully ending the crisis of violence largely depends on enabling people to develop technical and institutional skills and helping them to implement and manage development and investments in public and private sectors. In the long term development depends on improved services such as financing mechanisms to support investments in development projects and a sound development infrastructure in poor areas as a focus for human development. This is a continued partnership that involves a range of stakeholders and it is important that both developed and developing countries work together to provide decent living conditions for all.

The aim is to ensure that both external and internal development includes a performance plan in line with new development concepts and is well focused and reliable in order to achieve its goals. It is therefore mandatory for developing countries to improve their understanding of development and sustainable development issues and to clarify to themselves that the sound management of their natural resources is a prerequisite for the achievement of sustainable development. Future policy decision making should be informed by the fact that developing countries' economies and the livelihoods of their people depend on fair play, an open market and foreign policies that no longer put developing countries under pressure from unsustainable development.

Furthermore, the challenge is also on developing countries to utilise natural resources to develop their economies while at the same time conserving the environment to avoid the adverse impacts of pollution, soil erosion, deforestation and general degradation. Each institution's role and responsibility for national development involves monitoring the maintenance and protection of the environment and providing guidance on appropriate actions, which compels the country to produce a report on its activities in this area every two years. The development of the report receives support from the development banks in industrialised countries, and various national governments in developing countries, all under the institutional oversight and execution of effective management control.

Such an approach enables various critical development issues to be identified, as well as the driving forces that put pressure on the environment, and indicates the impact of evolving policy and legislative responses in mitigating the challenges of development. If developing countries want to achieve the objectives of long-lasting peace and political stability through development growth, this will send a message that sound development is making the right choice on the basis of up-to-date and reliable information. This is all related to the question of inefficiency in leadership. It has to be realised that long-lasting external control faces constraints caused by the deeper influence of governments' inability to maintain high standards and qualified employees. Instead, a combination of local poor management from the top, either caused by partisan influence or nepotism, results in inefficiency in local leadership.

This combination of inefficiency and economic constraints is of course a challenge in terms not only of reducing external influence but also for providing local leadership and a sufficient standard of services. It is frustrating and difficult to accept the slowness and inefficiency of a completely different culture. Lack of development is not necessarily to do with external policies alone but a reflection of both external and local government's internal political miscalculations as well as mismanagement of the economy. Nevertheless, it is also inextricably linked with theories related to developed countries' foreign policies hidden in a form of a subculture based in control through racial superiority ethnocentric theory control.

Examining the divisive cultural context of beliefs within the broader world development market shows, in a way that connects to both the past and the present, that industrial Western countries need to question many of the assumptions about their belief in superiority that may be identified as discriminatory. Our theoretical framework shapes our beliefs about superiority, but the most important thing to realise is that we have no choice over the race or culture into which we are born.

The argument is that if I am born white, I am more likely to be privileged than is a black child born in Africa, although I am not biologically superior to the child born in Africa. What I am trying to explain is that there is no evidence that people of a particular colour or origin are inherently aggressive or inferior, or that their identity, culture and self-esteem are less important, or that their views and feelings should be sidelined or ignored. Jensen in 1969, when trying to justify the genetic theory, saw intelligence as defined by what is measured in IQ tests. However, Jensen's use of IQ fell short of qualifying the fact that differences between average IQs could statistically have been classified through genetic rather than environmental contributing influences (Townsend 1971; Figueira (1974) and Coard (1971) -African Caribbean children being over - represented in ESN schools).

Genetic theory based on IQ tests was heavily contested by the Bay Area Black Psychology Association, which challenged the practice of using IQs test in a San Francisco court, claiming that they degraded black students as mentally retarded and excluded them from classes for gifted students (Cfr, Edwards (1978) Students teachers rated taped recorded W.I children speaking in Creole dialect as having the least academic potent). Nevertheless, claims of superiority can be identified as persistent beliefs arising out of psychological feelings of threat on the part of some privileged minorities in positions of authority who want to maintain these theories and beliefs and discriminate against those who were not 'one of us'.

Apart from the obvious factor of social deprivation, little is known about how racism as an inner feeling directly or indirectly affects all races. In applying Piaget's theory, psychologists diagnosed low achievement as a result of 'insufficiently structured intellectual setting or from cognitive defects - arising from insufficient age appropriate stimulation' (Cfr. (Ausubel 1964, Bloom et al 1965, Deutech et al 1967, Hunt 1967). The theoretical definition of racism according to Brooks says that:

*The cause of prejudice is seen as lying in the individual. It is an essentially psychological, irrational phenomenon, originating in individual inadequacies. On the other hand, antipathy as an attitude is arrived at in a rational way, and the cause lies in the object of the aggression or in the attitudes of this kind are culturally and socially transmitted, whereas prejudice is not (*Brooks, D., (1975). Race and Labour in London Transport, Oxford University Press, p.14*).*

The racism we see today is an outgrowth of slavery and European colonial expansion. Racism was heavily practised during colonialism and subsequently the greatest enemy of developing countries has been disunity and a low level of political and developmental integration. That is why these countries have suffered from the nightmare of developmental slavery for 300 years. Therefore, based on these grounds racism is no longer tied to the ideological notion of inequality in racial identity, which is the root of dominance. This forms part of a post-modern policy of differences practised by a whole range of neo-colonialist ideological movements.

In the first instance, there are three aspects of wider use racism that are recognised as inextricably related to national and external foreign policy based on the dominance of power and are continually reinforced in the current political world. The implications of local policies are cited in the case of the racism those from ethnic minorities face in employment, which in the past would have been represented by a direct attack on coloured people, even blaming them for things they had not done. Reports indicate that racism is still an endemic problem in society, although it has shifted from physical attacks to undermining coloured employees' ideas and suggestions. Others would argue that the basis of employment must make clear the acceptable treatment of ethnic minorities and protect the rights of coloured people. So the assumption of an obligation is an important element in employment law.

I have chosen to concentrate on UK law for two principal reasons. First, there is a difference between UK and European law, leading to differences in the way they treat people from developing countries, in some instances leading to differential treatment of coloured people. Secondly, it would not be wise to compare UK immigrants with immigrants to the USA, because UK immigrants are still finding their way in the process of full integration, despite the fact that there is a third generation in some cases, compared to the result of America's long cultural struggle, which is that each culture is celebrated as vital for unity.

In the UK we still believe that we are a law-abiding people and not many managers deliberately set out to defy the law. Nevertheless, obedience of legal requirements, though necessary, is not sufficient for the creation of equal opportunity. The law provides the essential foundation; only positive management action designed to suit the needs of each particular enterprise can put flesh and blood on the legal bones (Brooks, D., (1975). Race and Labour in London Transport, Oxford University Press; Sear, 1981:294).

In 1991 British cabinet minister Mr Jackson described racism as 'harmful, wrong and also wasteful (Jackson in Newham Recorder, 24th January 1991) He was not talking about racism in employment or about the problem of coloured people living in the West, but about the racism inherent all sorts of social services. Coloured people find it harder to obtain the services they require, to the extent that whites living in predominantly coloured communities suffer as well. The UK's response to the problem of racism was to introduce the Race Relations

Act 1965, which forbids any use of racial insults. In this Act, 'racial hatred' means hatred against of persons in society defined by reference to colour, race, nationality (including citizenship) or ethnic or national origins(Public Order Act 1986, part 111). Under the Act it is supposed to be an offence to use any language of insult, threatening, abusive or behaviour or displaying any written material that is threatening to any 'ethnic' group. It also became an offence to incite racial hatred where it could be proved that the intention was to stir up such hatred. Because of the difficulty of proving intent, the law was amended by the Race Relations Act 1976, which replaced the requirement of intent with an objective test. It became enough that the defendant's conduct was likely to stir up racial hatred, whether or not that was what he or she intended.

On the other hand, the fact that there was a law does not mean that racism was stamped out of society. Racism was forbidden in public use and there was also the promotion of equal opportunities in employment. Nevertheless, the success of this is also debatable, as there is no one to police it or to observe how many black people's applications for jobs are turned down everyday on the grounds of race.

In fact, it is arguable that through the use of the law racism was simply driven underground. It still exists in society as much as ever, although in the public domain it is not officially acceptable. Another aspect of racism is foreign policy, in which the fundamental problem lies in two main areas: first, investing in areas only where there is the possibility of exploiting natural resources; secondly, the pattern of arms sales. The role of the military is a major factor in foreign and defence policies, which are dominated by profiteering from the sale of arms. Despite the fact that many developed countries deny selling arms to undemocratic states, they use the proceeds for such sales to the benefit of their own citizens. For several decades European countries have been the largest defence exporters in the world after the USA, and evidence shows that they have even supplied countries that known to use arms against dissident citizens. Take the example of refugee camps in DR Congo, where it was discovered that European countries had supplied the Inteharamwe militia of Rwanda and enabled it to invade Rwanda for a second massacre.

In order to get to grips with the dilemma of being black, whether you are living in your own country or in the West, several points need to be considered: the way in which the theory of racism has been embedded right from colonial days and still reappears in foreign policies; discriminatory development market policies and practices; political dominance of poor countries by sales of arms to developing countries to use for terrorising their own people in order to fulfil foreign interests and for the agents using them to remain in power. Equally, it must be acknowledged that among coloured races there is an extreme diversity of selfish groups whose focus and interests are their personal gain at the expense of the wider population.

This is the crucial question in why Africa is always seen as being in political crisis, in particular in relation to the term 'colour' because blacks are seen as never being united. Clearly, the last 50 years of constant political insecurity have been a major challenge at a time in which industrial developed nations continued to consolidate their commercial predominance. It is therefore important to understand whether this unique situation of past colonial influence is a good or bad thing; development politics cannot be explained without taking into account all these factors. The only positive argument here is that if blacks can unite and identify mutual needs, they must approach the issue of ending the culture of relying on aid and grants, which is the culture that has held them back from developing.

A successful approach to development needs to take into account a whole range of institutional, social and structural issues. Economists often point to the lack of liberalisation in international trade policies and a refusal to accept protectionism in an open market framework as factors that fail to facilitate an open economy and trade to improve participation in development.

Under these social conditions, there is an often-repeated assertion that the lack of economic development in developing countries has led many young people to radical extremist beliefs. Various voices are concerned that exclusion and divisive policies are not only pervasive but nor are they accidentally imposed by powerful countries. If conceived in this way they are situational, representing dominant economic interests, suggesting that the issue of a lack of civilisation is not a carefully weighed moral argument, but rather a political weapon to be used to suit the needs of the dominant force. While all these were characteristics of colonisation and the establishment of self-interests, they have continued to cripple the ability of developing countries to avoid accepting dependency on developed countries.

What is relevant in this instance is to argue for the strategic need for a firmer and binding global law protecting human rights and placing pressure on all countries to pursue ethical foreign policies. So often the major guarantors of peace and loudly heard advocates of democracy actually lead to unethical foreign policies that promote human rights. What is discussed here is viewed as a possible way of controlling the influence of all these ill-defined policies that stem from the belief in superiority and impose economic dominance or are a form of decolonising poor countries. Ironically, all the claims of underachievement emanate from the lack of a desire to change.

The issue of ethical arms sales demonstrates nicely a major dilemma in industrial countries' use of ideological foreign policies. These policies blindly accept that various dictators are unable even to demand a unifying international law for the open market because there is no unanimity among developing countries to challenge policies of exploitation. There is some recognition of a preference for the tokenistic subsistence of grants or development aid for a real desire for poorer countries to engage in development. This is part of the reason discriminatory foreign policies are never likely to change, because the system tends to favour those in power. The fear of dictatorial leaders who favour a closed market is that if the world market is open, it may provide opportunities for more people to become richer; this reflects the belief that a richer society is uncontrollable.

However, the general view of the public and opposition politicians is that poverty results from the neglect by the ruling party in order to punish those who don't support government policies. In many cases, in the areas where there are more supporters of the ruling party people are better off than those who elected representatives from other political parties. It is possible that political agents benefit from the use of foreign financial support as a useful piece of political rhetoric, especially for use during the election campaign. It should be the direct concern of both local politicians and worldwide leaders to take responsibility for defending the poor in development policies.

Poverty eradication policies

Politics is about society and therefore about people. Sadly, since colonial times political society has been corrupt and is still the major factor in the downfall of developing countries' leaderships, particularly when they are ousted by a coup, and either tribalism or partisan favouritism always accompanies the corruption. Sociologically, politics can be described as the social organisation or maintenance of society and people's daily actions. Therefore, politics has to promote the cohesion of society, neutralising forces of disintegration and providing an overall framework for people's actions and the division of labour in society, which explains things that are happening and why they have to happen.

Tracing the history of politics in developing countries shows that the politics, development superstructure and education systems that were introduced after independence were inadequate and did not provide a basis for long-term development, leading to decline instead. The education was too theoretical and only promoted colonial interests rather than the systems, structures and functions that were needed. This is why there are still many challenges in changing the patterns of social and organisational regulations. In other words, learning is not only seeking to understand how society functions, but to go one step further to determine how theories and policies can be implemented and are achievable.

I will go further to qualify what I am saying and state that the reason African developing countries have had serious problems regarding development is that when they obtained independence the majority of educated black people had only acquired theoretical knowledge without practical experience. This was a serious problem, because even just to run a factory they had either to depend on expatriates or the Indians who had worked as assistants to white colonialists. The black men had not been trained for the jobs (literally the emphasis of man) and there were only a few black women employees in factories during the early days of colonialism.

In colonial days black people either worked as porters or guards of factories and of their white masters' homes, or in the military, and those who were educated were employed in white-collar jobs, mainly as clerical assistants simply entering figures and filing. In those days having a job was regarded as a great achievement. For instance, factories were run and maintained by whites and Asians who had been brought especially to East Africa to construct railway lines and chose to remain after these countries' independence. When the dictatorship regimes in some countries like the former Zaire under Mubutu and Idi Amin in Uganda, the factories ceased to function, because those who took them over were unable to manage them effectively. Today what you see is railway lines covered by bush. National leadership had also fallen into the hands of political activists who did not have any public office experience. Their first mistake was employing unqualified family members, relatives, tribes people and fellow political activists who supported them remaining in power. In some cases, where leadership survived being ousted it was either through dictatorial rule, or the fear of arrest of any opposition by police and military force to crush any political revolts. This is how violence became part of the culture of rulers and kept them in power. This type of leadership cultivates a deep-rooted culture of corruption and inducement to bribery. It is argued that with this sort of corrupt system, it does not matter how strong the national forces are or how many natural resources a country may have, it is still heading for disaster.

I would go further and claim that political corruption subverts development by leading to the misuse of resources in buying weapons and keeping a huge military force, which are further sources of developmental failure. This should not create the impression that all leaders are naturally corrupt, but that another political problem arises somewhere within the leadership system. The head of state may be above corruption yet be know that some of their most powerful supporters are corrupt. Nevertheless, they would be aware that coming down heavily on such people would be committing political suicide, since their interest is to keep in power, and the only option is to turn a blind eye to corruption.

Therefore, the culture entrenched in developing countries follows the line that corruption is a normal and acceptable part of business dealings, from government officials to ordinary farmers. There is even a saying in Africa when someone is appointed to high office: 'So and so has fallen into things.' Everyone knows that you give a bribe to a clerical officer to find your file and that you have to bribe traffic officers to drive freely, whether you are at fault or not. In most cases those who see beyond the cultural boundaries of corruption are religious leaders or academics that are not interested in challenging the political system, either out of fear for their own safety or because they see no purpose in spending their time and energy on something that will not change tomorrow. Some academics who are successful in having their voices heard can actually be manipulated with possibilities of promotion by being forced into being part of the system that implements the political agenda.

Furthermore, genuine consultation means involving all political parties in drafting plans, and modifying, implementing and revising them on the basis of their effectiveness in practice. If those managing the country's development are not willing to involve all party politicians and community leaders at all stages, consultation becomes a meaningless exercise. There is also another inherited factor in the politics used in former colonies, as the structure was often designed in such a way that subjects had to be submissive to authority, an approach that indirectly operated to facilitate foreign interests and the protection of dictatorship. The concept of universal justice requires the misuse of power to be reviewed where it seems that some individuals or groups are trying to resist unjust laws. This may mean that abuse of human rights is occurring in various forms, such as unlawful imprisonment or violent mistreatment by law enforcers. This is how dictators terrorise the opposition when political groups try to oppose the bad policies of the ruling regime. Analysts note that in undemocratic systems, particularly dictatorships, such groups have very little influence on their governments when they attempt to challenge policies and ensure that public needs are not marginalised.

Chapter three

The fate of developing countries

Impact of bad policies

The last chapter stressed the importance of liberating developing countries by explaining economic policies and factors that have hindered development due to the fact that they hinge on foreign interests that make local interests harder to achieve. It is also vital to unravel the social control ethos underpinning the fact that the exclusion of developing countries from the world market is an obstacle to their development. The main purpose of this chapter is to shed light on how foreign policies going as far back as the eighteenth century are applied racially through dominant theories and are seen as the root of conflict. In particular, Western influence has continued in developing countries and has continued to fail them, which is why this chapter needs to show the predicament that these countries are facing.

The history of the human race is not merely a history of events or a chronology of occurrences; it always has the objective of survival. The modern concern is with development in both developed and still developing countries, but there is an inability to develop within the architecture of social control. At the same time, developing countries face greater challenges in terms of the implications of ideological policies for their economic exclusion. According to sociologists, society is a site of conflict in which multiple interest groups compete with one another for scarce resources. The history of all cultures seems to have developed to a point where people treasure and have pride in the cultural achievements of their own group and correspondly are derogatory towards other groups. Nevertheless, the freedom to encourage economic activities to take place demands stability and peace in which people can plan and execute their ideas in the hope of a better future.

However, regarding to the question of development with the daily accompaniment of a violent political crisis, if the history of the causes of our contemporary political crisis is looked at in more detail, it is fundamental to ask development is possible in such a situation of politics that are not conducive for liberation. Given that the development and determination of policies are controlled by industrial developed nations, there is therefore a need to trace the dominant development policies of social exclusion, of all which might be based on a belief in the importance of subordinating other nations. The issues involved need, if possible, to be assessed against the needs to which they are the answer and the impact on coloured races' determination of their underachievement. This is the kind of theory that was derived from the ideas of racism under early colonial rule.

The theory of racism seems to have been developed into a desire for the dominance of coloured people. Where political conflicts and poverty exist in developing countries, these are partly blamed on the unjust policies of discriminatory Western countries. We may as well define the dominance culture theory as the prejudice and practice of disadvantaging or advantaging those of one race solely on the grounds of their colour. The idea of a link between inherited physical traits and certain personality traits, such as intellect and culture coupled with achievement within it, is a fallacious theory that develops the arrogant stereotypes that one group of people are inherently superior to other races. Such superficial beliefs make it clear why racism needs appropriate instruments to combat it and why it is a threat and still a hindrance in some areas for diversity and unity, as the human race keeps endangering its reasonable ability to fight racism.

The Holocaust, in which the Nazis systematically sent untold numbers of Jews, gypsies, Slavs and members of other ethnic groups to their deaths, was a terrifying reminder of the human potential for destruction, and the consequences of Weber's theory of the 'iron cage' of modernity gone mad. Racism is like a virus in the human body, which directly attacks the structure of development and disabling its function by consolidating the power of direct rule. It is for this reason that African countries are stuck and lack the ability to develop within a holistic perspective that combats the long-term policies that have kept the continent on its knees and pushed it into deeper crises of unceasing civil conflict.

Several voices express the concern that Western countries must relate their own development to that of the rest of the countries in the world in numerous practical ways. This emphasis derives from the Christian teaching of love your neighbour as you love yourself, and is equated with regard for fellow human beings to reverse exploitative development structures. The evidence of this is the failure to end discriminatory foreign policies that heighten local conflicts by a whole series of related worldwide political interests in Western countries.

This point illustrates developing countries' struggle to recover from colonialism and post-war black emigration, and includes the decisive role of Islamic militant uprisings in the form of suicidal martyrdom in reshaping the political agenda of world politics; this will be developed later. Industrial nations must abolish inappropriate policies that create situations like the one in the jungles of DR Congo or nearly two decades of war in northern Uganda that have left thousands dead and over two million people displaced, in order to stop the exodus of refugees and emigrants seeking sanctuary in developed nations.

In my opinion it is possible for the world slowly to revolve in the right direction, where a dreamer can dream of a liberated world where people are able to live in peace, when gun factories will be converted to make agricultural machinery and tractors to produce food for the starving people of the world. But developed nations will first have to address the issue of greedy politicians who subject millions of people in developing countries to act as agents for discriminatory policies. It is a moral failure on the part of the West that coloured nations have been unable effectively to eradicate racism in a wider context.

Unjust practices must be disentangled from foreign policies for the implantation of an effective equilibrium in the worldwide development of the human race, where one world will focus on the development of the rule of peace and stability. Since there is no basis whatever in politics or development for any race to believe that they are in any way intrinsically superior to other races, it is imperative for developed nations to stop treating African people as nothing more than animals who excel at killing each other.

The current political crisis highlights the dilemma faced by refugees when military rebel groups rampage through and loot their villages, and even refugee settlements are unsafe for most people. Human Rights Watch calls the crisis a humanitarian disaster, repeatedly referring to the fact that civilians are in the crossfire. Most refugees are forced to flee their homes on more than one occasion, and many have lost relatives or neighbours to the ongoing fighting among various rebel factions and an untrained and resource-poor national army. Refugees are used as human shields by different factions of guerrilla groups. Rebel groups often prevent civilians from closing the border to leave these groups directly exposed to their enemies.

Another fear is that the local government has neither the ability nor the resources to house so many refugees, especially elderly and weaker refugees who are reluctant to leave the transit camp. Another serious concern that to some extent force many parents to stay near the border is in case the fighting subsides and they can return to their homes in the hope of reuniting with their surviving family; children get separated from their parents while fleeing violence in their village and have to hope to eventually find them.

One would have thought that the Holocaust presented a lesson to the world, but such horrible massacres have occurred in Rwanda, in former Yugoslavia, Kenya and right now in DRC; the region also has major conflicts that need to be addressed, such as those in Somalia, Ethiopia, Eritrea, Djibouti, the Democratic Republic of Congo and Sudan. In relation to the conflict in Gaza, the Archbishop of Canterbury called on Jews, Muslims and Christians to unite, and urged 'all those who have the power to halt this spiral of violence to do so. Those raising the stakes through the continuation of indiscriminate violence seem to have forgotten nothing, and learned nothing.' Without a serious international initiative to achieve peace, he said, 'the future for the Holy Land and the whole region is one of more fear, innocent suffering, and destruction' (The Church Times, the Church of England Newspaper, January 2009).

Evidence such as this only confirms that, as long as elements of racism persist and there is a re-emergence of anti-Semitism in European countries where people are still struggling for recognition, these are the consequences of a unitary politics of 'race'. However, American society, which sometimes is referred to as an evil empire, has spoken more loudly with one decisive move for change. Despite mixed reactions, white and African Americans alike celebrated the election of the first African American president of the United States of America as a sign of liberation for all her citizens.

However, it would be wise to wait for African celebrations for two reasons. First, Africa has previously had its own son at the United Nations as a General Secretary, but he did virtually nothing for Africa, not even to save one million Tutsis during the massacre in Rwanda. Second, Obama's leadership might lead to a re-convergence of post-colonial discrimination and post-modernist discriminatory extremism in a new cultural politics of modernisation. This may lead to a resurgence of popular support for racist organisations such the National Front and Nazi groups, which are still scattered all over Europe.

As much as I wish him well in his leadership, from the African point of view the continent should wait to see which policies Obama will support, as there two types of foreign policies that promote justice and reduce injustice. Three important aspects of development are raised by academia. The first is increasing people's income and the consumption levels of food, shelter and clothing, medical services and education. Second is creating conditions conducive to the growth of people's self-esteem through the establishment of structures that promote human dignity and respect. Third is increasing people's freedom to choose.

The main implication of the current crisis cannot be limited to merely quantifiable indicators, since it is a normative concept that embraces socio-development, political and cultural variables that are also non-quantifiable. This may be the exercise of lack of choice or it may be that bias in the system excludes developing countries from pursuing development in their economic structures and instead directs them into the political conflict caused by a few available resources. Brookfield summarises this clearly as follows: 'The popular trend is to define development in terms of progress towards a complex of welfare goals of human development, such as reduction of poverty and unemployment and diminutions of inequality (Brookfield, 1975:3). This suggests that to reduce the level of an underclass in the form of development policies, some basic factors will stop the support of political agents in developing countries where the dominant political policies hinge on racially differential treatment under the rule of law and development has created a political situation surrounded with fear, threat, hatred, corruption and violence to silence their opponents.

Such a definition clearly depicts the idea of structural changes in the system, which demands a response that may facilitate an open process of social justice in developing countries. One cannot talk about development without mentioning its sister concept, growth. Johnson defined growth as 'an increase in total output or an increase in resource with which to produce total output' (Johnson, 1983:9). To understand the nature of the game you have to look at many other examples of the use of law to restrict a particular group, while the same law allows another group to dominate. The whole history of coloured people reflects this relationship.

Although evidence of past and present dealings reveals that judges' approach to racial justice and equality in law has changed over the years, it still demands an overhaul of discrimination within the national and international legal system. Justice is often personified as a blindfolded woman holding the scales of justice and a sword. The blindfold symbolises that justice is blind to individuals (Johnson, 1983:9) and suggests that all people are equal before the law. The sword represents the judgment and enforcement of the law.

Thus it is argued that the notion of formal equality underlies the rule of law, and if the rule of law were to be acceptable in Rwandan society, for instance, it would signify the country's return to the vital features of equality for all before the law. To establish justice through the rule of law would mean justice applied equally and the idea of the rule of law is preserving society (Ibid.). Johnson's definition stops halfway and does not take into consideration the horizontal spread of resources. Thus, growth is measured in aggregated terms, for instance as Gross National Product. It is therefore further argued that growth is a precondition for development. This view agrees with Mosher's observation that without growth no amount of income distribution, no sentimental concern for the less well-off in poor societies, can have much effect (Mosher, 1970:3).

Another reflection of my emphasis on development growth grounded on good leadership may therefore be defined as the aggregate of society's production of goods and services over time, and is usually measured in terms of Gross National Product or per capita income. Simon Kurnets defines growth as 'a long term rise in the capacity to supply increasingly diverse development goals and goods to its population, this growing capacity based on diversity policies and advanced technology and the institutions and ideological arguments that it demands (Cf. Kurnets, 1971:17).

In the bad sense of development, however, humankind becomes overcome by the greed for wealth and although he goes and succeeds in acquiring wealth, his character, his integrity and his very soul can become mortgaged to wealth. Where people cease to have control over themselves and their wealth, they have acquired it in the wrong way. In this context, the quality of life refers to the way in which people are making use of things, not how much they possess or how much they acquire and consume.

A new political twist in development between Rwanda, France and Germany shows that the law is still used as discriminatory tool to treat coloured nations differentially in terms of diplomatic immunity.

African Parliamentary Union (APU) members have called for the unconditional release of Rose Kabuye, a senior Rwandan official arrested in Germany. As New Times Rwandan Newspaper stated, 'By virtue of the principle of equal sovereignty of all the members of the United Nations Organisation, abuse of the principle of international law constitutes, not only a violation of the sovereignty of a country like Rwanda... but also a violation of the principle by which a country cannot exercise its power over the territory of another.' Rwanda explicitly rejected France's claim to jurisdiction over the incident and called for a judicial settlement before the International Court of Justice. France failed to consent to the jurisdiction of the Court (New Times, Monday 1st December 2008).

Austin Ejiet vividly highlights another example of legal differentiation in diplomatic status, which speaks volumes: *In the mid 1970s a White British teacher trainer then based at the National Teachers College, Kyambogo, one Dennis Cecil Hills, wrote and published a book about president Idi Amin's government, titled The White Pumpkin. In the book he had described the president as a village tyrant with a keen peasant wit. Somebody picked on that phrase and told the president that some "Zionist" and "Imperialist" had insulted him* (New Vision, Tuesday 23

November 2008). The author was arrested, tried by a military tribunal and sentenced to die by firing squad. Concerted global diplomatic efforts were made to save Hills. Britain sent no less a person than foreign secretary James Callaghan to plead the author's cause. Even the Pope made rare representations to the Kampala government to save Mr Hills, which is what finally happened (New Vision, Tuesday 23 November 2008).

Thus coloured people's human life and values are cheapened. The International Criminal Court's uncompromising search for justice in Africa – in places such as northern Uganda, ravaged by the Lord's Resistance Army (LRA), Central African Republic (CAR), the Democratic Republic of Congo (DRC) and Sudan's Darfur region – has startled many observers. The recent move by the prosecutor of the International Criminal Court (ICC), Luis Moreno Ocampo, seeking the indictment of Sudanese President Omar is not unwarranted, as many voices are heard wondering where such an order comes without a shred of local evidence of what exactly people are looking for as a means to end the crisis.

Of course, the ICC could have consulted politicians, but politicians have their own political agenda and are less concerned with ordinary people. This is severely endangering people's lives and simply prolonging the conflict, rather than bringing about a peaceful end to the violence. Africa comprises societies that are accustomed to restorative justice approaches. The fear of ICC prosecution might scare indicted parties from engaging in meaningful peace negotiations. Some people affected by the LRA insurgency in northern Uganda, for example, blame the ICC for their continued plight, and some for those who referred the conflict situations in their countries to the ICC have themselves committed international war crimes in the past.

We can also look at how the law is discriminatorily employed to exclude coloured people, which provides the legal framework within which industrial nations can easily exploit the system of former colonies as buyers and sellers of goods and services without showing their face in the whole exploitative mechanism. International principles developed from the resolution of disputes concerning foreign diplomats under their constitutional laws, therefore arresting a diplomat with immunity breaches international agreements and undermine the sovereignty of the individual state. Such an indictment only confirms how former colonies are still subjected to former colonisers according to their foreign policies, and diplomatic immunity only protects those who serve foreign interests. As Hans Kelsen put it: 'The law is an order, and therefore all legal problems must be set and solved as order problems. In this view of the definition of the legal structural analysis of positive law, it must be free of all ethical political value judgements (Kelsen, H., 1991:430-431). In this way diplomatic immunity theoretically becomes a political value that only protects foreign leaders when they are serving foreign interests.

If this is so, it is then an abrogation of intended diplomatic values when the law turns out to promote discrimination that treats diplomats from developing countries as an underclass and creates a two-tier service. We do not seek the supremacy of the coloured race but rather a world in which all members of the human race can be treated equally under the rule of law.

To uphold human rights values means to stop funding regimes that violate freedom of speech and the right to life. This book argues that a valuable tool in the liberation of poor people is to eradicate the violent cultural systems of coloured leadership that rule with terror in their governance of the people, using political instability as a means of keeping themselves in power for ever. This book attempts to look at the use of violence within the religious context of morality to distinguish violence as a symptom of an abnormal condition and a result of human reactions to specific social conditions that reflect dysfunctional and abnormal societal circumstances.

Which situation best explains this 'inter-relationship' theory and expresses the nature of the violence and crime used to suppress the rights of minorities or even the majority is some cases? What happens today is related to what happened centuries ago under colonialism, which is seen by those affected as the controversial effects of racism or ethnic violence, which has existed for centuries as a problem and keeps reappearing in various forms of practice and causes the victimisation of other races. It is the important question of societal victims and grievances that discounts the claims of civilisation to argue that despite scientific achievements and the advancement of knowledge, violence is still as prevalent as ever in society and is likely to continue in the near future if world leaders choose to ignore it and fail to work in partnership to address concerns surrounding radical militants.

To avoid anarchy and to restrain industrial countries' domination of developing countries, the built-in checks and balances of the development structure need to be enhanced. In fact, what appears in all these developments challenges the claims of poor countries for any dream for development if discriminatory policies remain in use, destabilising the continent with the supply of arms. It also begs the question of where civilisation lies in all this. However, what seems to be different between the violence in poor countries and that in rich countries is the way that violence is committed and its speed or scale.

This raises another question, about the violence committed by developed nations dumping their weaponry as a form of greed, promoting the interests of development at the expense of human lives. In Somalia, whose guns have created a state of anarchy and made the country ungovernable?

If these groups have nowhere to obtain weapons, the whole approach to the general rules and principles that can be used as guidance in a particular crisis could be controlled by dynamic regional organisations such as permanently stationed United Nations or Organisation of African Unity forces, similar to the NATO force in Europe. Situations of political crisis and ethnic conflict change, sometimes very rapidly, and such a force would represent an effort to provide the best possible appropriate response to the tensions arising in the region. For example, there is a need for such an army to deal with Kenyan warlords at the next general elections (Jerry Okungui, Thursday, 13th November, 2008).

If charitable and humanitarian organisations keep silent about atrocities inflicted on a population caught up in political conflict, it is a betrayal of the international community. Foreign international humanitarian organisations working in developing countries have recently been blamed in the DR Congo region for a failure to expose brutal governments to the world or to identify what has happened as an infringement of human rights before it is too late. These double standards have led to millions being butchered and left on their own to die without a voice. Many people felt angry as a result of the escalated wider war crisis which is seen by many young people in economic deprived areas both in developing and developed countries as ignoring the peril of poor people and the very high risk — which history should have taught us — the very high risk of financial stringency leading to political extremism. This is argued as the source of the anger finding its expression in xenophobia, prejudice, rivalry — all the tactics that both sociologists and psychologists remark on as the displacement of unease and fear.

Of course, it is understood how hard it is to convince the victims or survivors of political conflicts who witnessed massacres like those in Rwanda, Bosnia or other parts of the world that revenge, the use of violence and killing is anything but wrong. Wars and conflicts leave behind traumatised and impaired people, unable to fend for themselves yet discriminated against by both relatives and state authorities. Many years on, victims and survivors of human rights violations still bear the scars of these violations and little has been done to ensure that they have access to effective reparations to address their continued suffering and help them to rebuild their lives. In some cases they never recover, as a new discovery of information about their loved ones causes survivors to break down.

For instance, Bernard Jack Vogel '*ad tried to escape from a Nazi prisoner-of-war camp, but the details were sketchy. Martin was so devastated after the war; he didn't ask too many questions. But as time passed, his thoughts often drifted to his brother. "A month doesn't go by that it doesn't come up in the course of my own thoughts," said Martin Vogel, now 82. "But to me, it's always there: What if this? Why didn't he do this? And what happened to him? And that's what bothered me." The Boston resident read an article last week on CNN.com about Anthony Acevedo, a World War II medic who was among 350 U.S. soldiers held in a Nazi slave camp called Berga and der Elster, where dozens of soldiers were beaten, starved and killed. Less than half survived captivity*' (CNN International CNNA. Com/living /20/11/2008).

Victims just have to learn every day how to cope with their mental suffering. As we can see above, even survivors of the Jewish Holocaust still say that they continue to experience mental suffering to the present day. A desire for revenge is driven by the anger of the victim, and a subjective sense of feeling injustice which pays no respect to standards of evidence, proof and proportionality and therefore tends to lead to further injustices and to another spiral of violence and revenge.

The UN is increasingly becoming meaningless and irrelevant in developing countries when considering the failure to honour the ideas of its formation, which were to prevent any excessive use of violence. Now millions are being killed worldwide while its staff are disarmed by powerful nations whose interests must be considered first before human lives. UN is also seen as a club that caters for the interests of rich nations: when they need it, they will use it, but when they don't need it they will ignore UN decisions and do what meets their interests. Another weakness is that when the UN sends military protection for civilians, it is always overpowered by the national army and rendered ineffective. In my opinion if humanitarian projects were run locally and on a voluntary basis and there was no external funding, they would be doing a much better job.

In Rwanda, for example, the government auditor decided to refer the findings of a report from a local humanitarian organisation to the Supreme Court, after the report failed to indicate how leaders of Italia Solidale, a local church-affiliated NGO, diverted about Rwf 3 billion that had been meant for orphans. The NGO was established to help over 2000 orphans left vulnerable by the 1994 political conflict against the Tutsis. The report on the investigation observed that the NGO received substantial funding yet reflected very little work done on the ground to indicate how it was being used (New Times, Rwanda, and Sunday 7th December 2008).

Violence in developed nations is also on the increase, and new cases of political conflict are being reported. Violence is an endemic problem in the most affluent societies in the same way as in the remote jungles of Congo.

The international response is rarely appropriate and is usually only partial, consisting as it often does of a United Nations decision when the massacre has been carried out to provide aid to the few remaining survivors. A more appropriate response would be to provide aid in terms of raw materials, or to help developing countries learn the skills they need to develop their own industries and deliver excellent customer service. They need assistance from people with previous experience of working in a front-line customer-focused environment, as well as the ability to understand and avoid complex political issues and deliver strategic management services.

Two main reasons keep poor countries back from development. Evidence of a wider conspiracy often arises when local attempts are made to stop armed groups competing with various foreign arms dealers in the interests of supplying arms, for reasons clearly linked to profiting from conflict. This is equally related to the interests of multiple groups and can be argued as being caused by discriminatory foreign policies on the part of industrial countries, through their sales of arms. Secondly, the hunger for power of the local leadership only serves foreign interests and has resulted in one part of the world suffering for decades and being left in a decaying state of militia violence. Countries continue to be destabilised whenever an attempt is made to change leadership locally, which leads to a constant failure to restore peace.

This also reflects structural factors springing from leadership's failure to take the right strides towards development. They arm an opposition group to force the leadership to adhere to a discriminatory agenda, while on the other hand claiming how their countries are underachieving due to their black culture. All these are symptoms of a wider conspiracy and corruption caused by a lack of the capacity to liberate themselves. There is also a general failure to realise and recognise the fact that what affects one group of people, either in the jungles of Africa or in the deserts of the Middle East, will subsequently affect the rest of the world. These symptoms are hidden by the relatively favourable external foreign interests that have existed ever since colonialism. Thus, world leaders must realise that injustices to disfranchised groups result in violence and the loss of millions of human lives.

I wish to advance the theory that the world has failed to realise that the corruption of people's minds for power to keep others in control has created a state of dependence, and that a lack of development rationality undermines the claims of civilisation, which seem to lose their meaning when conventional social relations are under continual threat from the aggressiveness of others through deadly force. This violence and persecution have created local dictators who lack respect for human rights and tolerance of those with different views.

The political climate of violence in developing countries is recognisable in the fact that violence and dictatorship are coupled with threats that the principles of civilisation cannot ever achieve equilibrium or a stable world. Those who use violence will have to recognise that any denial of freedom of thought, expression or speech to other societies and a failure to take seriously the problems of millions of people trapped in a state of beggary while forcing them to succumb to foreign pressure will only keep circles of violence around the world. The use of violent means to liberate themselves will reappear until all races recognise each other and work together on equal terms.

Right now there are reports in the media of the possibility of a repeat of violence in DR Congo, the former Zaire. As an African my primary purpose is to focus on the widely recognisable fact that the south of the continent seems incapable of ending its problems of dictatorship, corruption and abuse of the rights of both individuals and groups, which keeps the entire population living under the bondage of fear, threat and the reality of violence, which have a profound impact on the lives of citizens.

Secondly, it reminds me of a little boy, Paul Kauma, who died at around 6 years old and was the son of the late David Kauma and the grandson of the spiritual leader and my godfather, Bishop Misaeri Kauma. Something special I remember about Paul was the way he detested violence. Each time he saw violence on the television he ran to his bedroom. Each time I hear and watch violence being committed around the world it reminds me of Paul, who seemed unique because other young boys like watching violent films and fights with powerful weapons, often identifying themselves with the winners as their heros. In my view all this simply promotes a violent society daily in our living rooms. It is my hope that this book will provide a stepping-stone to explain the danger of other forms of violence in our societies and initiate a debate about various cultural celebrations containing elements of violence, so that society can weed out any violent acts.

I also argue for education at an early age for young people and detecting where a challenge to bad behaviour is required, such as a bad attitude to work or leadership, before it develops into domestic violence. This is seen a way of early prevention within families before violence becomes a wider issue; it is a way of taking over the issues and information packs and generally raising awareness of the likelihood of developing oppression and its effects on society. Finally, it argues that too much dependence on a partisan quality of leadership is always subject to failure, where the problem is overlooking talents and capabilities outside political adherents in the civil service appointments, particularly in those appointed to responsibilities for developmental goals.

I sometimes wonder how far police training colleges or the military debate solutions to ending the use of violence in the hands of their junior staff, as it is often expected that the security agencies are ordinarily subordinate to the rule of law and should be seen to uphold it in society. It is disappointing to see police who are supposed to act as custodians of the values of law and order but choose to act in a contrary fashion and to make matters worse using violence. Consider a recent incident in Kampala when policemen mishandled a woman MP. The meaning of development is not necessarily the expansion of cities, but building a tolerant and inclusive society that respects the values of creation, where it is more important to build the human capacity to create an orderly society in which developmental activities are possible.

Another important part of the strategic approach to competence means well-trained people carrying out sound development policies, which regulate market forces and operate on the principle of transparency and accountability, in order to prevent corruption of the system, which is the root of violence. In order to control and prevent the system of power dominating in the form of repressive measures, which has been observed in recent events in different countries, it is relevant to compare the continued use of violence with wider examples of those who have taken radical actions to overcome developmental obstacles.

I hope to use real-life examples, issues and the latest findings from various developing countries, particularly those facing the difficulties of operating under foreign policies that disempower every effort made to implement local initiatives, according to evidence gathered in various development studies and observation of past performance. So while the findings are quite accurate, perhaps one or two areas need further explanation. It is further argued that leadership theories promoting non-violence always consider the wider scope of debates engaging in broad development as representing a variety of new ideas. In many countries under dictatorship the quality of leadership fosters people's fears through social ostracism, brainwashing, withholding information and dictatorial pronouncements coupled with threats. What is needed in the twenty-first century are three key strategies:

1. A consideration of contemporary local relationships and developmental needs. It is important to look at governance as providing a just system within a framework that allows people to be safely governed in a relationship of cohesion with no foreign dominance.

2. A request to industrial countries to recognise the developmental hindrance of the early exclusion of others. The pattern of colonial development is structured by implication on the use of law, but is actually used by the colonisers to subject the colonised and has maintained a position of developmental subjection. This is the reason for developmental strategies failing to be integrated and public participation being flawed.

3. A search for ways of creating the momentum that creates human development in correspondence with human rights.

These three strategic approaches are suggestions that will be dealt with later in more detail with compelling evidence, to demonstrate how strategy effectively can be changed to allow wider participation and to follow people's views. This is argued as the best way to avoid conflict and the use of violence. Whether you are dealing with staff, customers, investors or others, you first have to understand how people work and how new ideas catch on to appreciate what makes for successful leadership strategies.

Chapter four

Critical analysis of social development structures

The use of ethnocentric theories

This chapter cuts across the detail of the previous discussion to ask if the changes made in the last 50 years after independence in most developing countries have made any difference; indeed whether they have added up to a total transformation of the political scene in these countries. This chapter will also attempt to assess how far fundamental changes have been achieved in the social and humane conditions of ordinary people. Thus, the chapter asks whether the lack of overall development is related to what happens elsewhere. Most politicians like to present themselves as innovative and successful, but we don't have to take their assertions at face value.

It is therefore the intention of this chapter to evaluate a form of social organisation in the colonial period and to assess how the nature of modernity has developed violence in various forms as newly discovered social patterns in development measures applied in developed countries. The colonies were, of course, fuelled wholly by Western beliefs in superiority and dominance; however, colonialism has been on the political agenda for many generations. Colonial rule produced development, which in turn brought social and political tensions; after independence the political and trading system continued the process of dependence on the West that has transformed the world for better and for worse.

Globalisation through urbanisation, together with the expansion of mass communication, has made former colonies much more susceptible to new and radical ideas, whether good or bad. This is why the concern of this book is broadly posed at the beginning as a concern for violence, which is seen as the source of conflict, crisis and lack of development in poor countries. It is therefore argued that the idea of internationalisation or globalisation has wider implications, again both good and bad, where the bad presents one-sided manifestations and a lesser chance for the development of Third World countries around the world. Anything done in New York affects the rest of the world in a matter of hours, either through the mobility of people or the transmission of information, which has widespread ramifications for decision making.

Ironically, globalisation does not mean in reality what it seems to suggest in theory. Many poor countries struggle to engage in the process whereby each part of the world is linked in trade and communication. Critically, in developing countries globalisation only serves to provide information for consumerism and that is far as it reaches. In that case, globalisation is simply sensitising consumers to the growing links between, for instance, what we wear, the way we look, the way we eat and the car we drive. The tragedy is that the message is beamed into rich and poor countries alike, but not the idea that international trade policies are restricted by tariffs, custom duties or import quotas that are designed to protect the domestic economy from foreign competition. The question raised here is not an objection to the idea of consumerism (capitalism), but that the idea of globalisation must aim at both sides, not only halfway, which means taking the responsibility to address both the means and the purchasing power.

Later I will explore the question of differences in the interpretation of the causes of lack of development and political conflicts, using the political conflict in Rwanda as an example of how developing countries occasionally fail to grow developmentally in many areas. The main aim here is to provide the context for understanding the negative side of globalisation in the development of the use of violence, and highlight how from independence onwards there can be differences between interpretations of the political crisis. This can be traced to the settings of historical colonial, political and development structures, which were put in place deliberately. Such structures are seen as the source of political violence, which often resurfaces as tribal hatred; another interpretation suggests that these conflicts or tribal wars are political propaganda. The focus of this section will be to try to compare alternative claims and assess their validity. The general mood of cynicism is explored in relation to the reassertion of an agenda that embraces developmental change in addition to the development of pragmatic thinking about beliefs in superiority and theories of ethnocentrism that affected development in former colonies and prevents it to the present day. These social and ideological policies have served as a means of preventing institutions in developing countries from achieving effective change and are the basic parameter according to which political violence has increasingly dominated the military leadership of the developing nations. Therefore, the concept of development is rather hydra-headed, in that it can be approached from various fronts and disciplines. Just like the concept of religion, which is also difficult to define precisely, development is not easily defined or described as being this or that. This is simply because it cuts through many disciplines and several facets of life, such that the 'definitions are contextual and contingent upon the ideological, epistemological or methodological orientation of their purveyors' (David Simon & Anders Narman (eds), "Development as Theory and Practice", Harlow. Longmann, 1999, p.19).

This is why it is very difficult to give a precise answer to the question 'What is development?' Often, someone might be tempted to ask in response, 'What kind of development?' The implication is that within the scope of the argument in this chapter, I will focus on the socio-development of humans, where a definition of development cannot easily be found for its framework and direction, especially when it relates to development and conflict theories. It is for this reason that, at the centre of this chapter, I have decided to assess developing countries' colonial history to see whether the lack of development in developing countries is linked to the causes of political violence. Furthermore, it is argued that a proper perspective on the concept of development is imperative in order to allay the results of the failure of development in these countries. Goulet argues that authentic development must aim at the total realisation of human capabilities. The fact that development policies need to enhance the experience of marginalised people in developing countries cannot be left out as one of the factors to be taken into account.

Therefore, this chapter explores people's views about developing countries' social structures and focuses on criticisms from local respondents. I wish to argue that, if the objective of the colonial administration in developing countries was to create a superstructure, then it was obliged to ensure that all people were protected and secured 'from cradle to grave'. The consequences of this were far-reaching, characterised by developing countries producing what developing countries did not consume, yet consuming what they did not produce: exporting raw materials and importing finished goods.

It is also important to note that other influences were behind much that was happening in developing countries during colonial rule. The overall picture that emerges from the development of these negative observations suggests that ethnic distinctions were in the interests of developing countries. I can say that Maquet's assertion is discounted by the available evidence and is misleading, since before colonialism came to developing countries there was no differentiation among people. Findings borne out by a number of studies examined biological claims but instead highlight wider criticisms of colonial policies, which were identified as the source of conflict, embedded in development strategies and a dysfunctional developmental structure that creates human suffering, violence and the struggle of one people against another.

The idea of supremacy meant that the structure of colonial ideological development was associated with a psychological theory of supremacy hidden in the use of biological theory and opening the door to the creation of exploitative, stereotyping development structures. In relation to colonial development in developing countries, Berger and Luckmann's theory of how reality is constructed, ordered and maintained commits the familiar error of attempting to divorce the concept from the problem of the natural human fear of uncertainty.

Colonial development activity in developing countries, from a bi-focal point of view, concerned the definition of development structures that were not agreed by all. The empirical problem of measurement is argued as having led colonial rule to seek psychological development efforts (Berger Peter, 1966:104). So, for example, structural design incorporated ideas in an extreme form, approaches that concentrated on characteristics of the biological or psychological in the focus of developing countries' development structures.

Bankers in developing countries were led by capitalist interests to generate new theoretical perspectives that challenged developing countries' traditional established institutions. In practical terms, it is argued that this is why the colonial psychology around development interests became the colony's development reality. Because it operates through ethnocentric theories, the psychological fear that can be traced as being linked with colonial policies was designed to discriminate against developing countries, as such theories did not accommodate the circumstances of social groups or plans for long-term development.

This is why the theory or the construction of reality in colonial development is open to a number of criticisms (http://www.cpnm. org/new/English/articles_news/rootcause_karma.htm.). Michael Tedaro argues that development is 'the process of improving human lives' (Tedaro, M. P., 1977:6.). It is also argued that, having abolished developing countries' traditional system of alignment of the economy to cater for the social well-being of the population, it was important to provide 'tools to the pool' in order to promote future development management and avoid creating the mass unemployment that exists in developing countries today. In respect of human improvement, this chapter has argued that social changes were related to development interests in colonial people who had a greatly distorted view of relationships between people in developing countries. Three important aspects were raised by the developing countries' economists, suggesting that it was essential for colonial development to take the following steps The problem of the choice of development structure in developing countries and the refusal to engage developing countries in the interpretation of social development reality is argued by Lenski to be an ethnocentric belief, but one that provides a better explanation of the relationship between race and colonial development than that provided by earlier racist theorists (Lenski, G., Nolan, P., and Lenski, J., 1995:174). It is therefore argued that, in effect, the refusal amounted to privileging only colonisers as far as development was concerned. It was further argued that this was colonial discrimination of the highest order, as it lacked respect for developing countries. Respect is a fundamentally important quality for participation as a citizen and part of the human community (Interviews with Bankers at Kigali, August 1998).

The next chapter explores the question of differences in the interpretation of the causes of political conflict in developing countries. The main aim here is to try to highlight differences between interpretations of that conflict.

The source of violence

Considering the relevance of legitimising developing countries' cultural development structures suggests that the production of knowledge can be a collective and social process in a stronger and more active sense than Berger and Luckmann considered. The renewal of traditional structures was needed, not their abolition, providing liberation into responsibility for specific though limited aims in connection with the lives of people in developing countries and the needs of the static developmental sections of the population, notably children and old people.

Internationally standardised rules and regulations that aim to ensure that, in theory at least, all people are treated equally are either not available or not considered important in developing countries. On the other hand, it is argued that equality of treatment in the colonial administrations was necessary to offer opportunities for the emphasis to be placed on rules guaranteeing equality of treatment. The lack of local participation was seen as an infringement of people's rights. Any process that undervalues people and discounts their participation as a fundamental feature of its reality should be treated with profound suspicion. In fact, most people from developing countries have, as one, overwhelmingly argued that such the desire for equality should have been realised. will next explore the question of differences in the interpretation of the causes of political conflict in developing countries.

Some refer to the overall source of conflict as a problem of historical African tribal differences and hatred, others as differing party politics functioning as organs of ideologically like-minded and ethnic groups, while yet another interpretation of ethnic tensions is often argued by local people to be a regime of political propaganda. All these issues will be considered next to try to compare the sources of political crises. For instance, the views of journalists and of academia are compared to show how interpretations of developing countries' political conflict differ between local and foreign agencies. If one pursues the constructionist view of the development of developing countries' structures as being directly responsible for the colonial power of dominance, the process unveils strategies for perpetuating capitalist interests and exploitation on a wider scale. Furthermore, it is argued that a proper perspective on the concept of development is imperative in order to allay the result of failure of development in developing countries. Thus, development must be seen as building up people so that they can forge a future for themselves.

Denis Goulet is a rare development scholar who provides a crystal-clear concept of development. He argues that authentic development should aim at the total realisation of human capabilities. Promoting a positive methodology, he further adds that 'development is simply a means to the human ascent... all humanity is viewed as receiving a summons to assume its own identity' (Goulet, Denis, (1971). The Cruel Choice: A New Concept in the Theory of Development, Centre for the study of development and social change, New York: Atheneum, pp. 295-312). Criticism of the classic colonial social theorist's drive for development rationality, which appeared to be the main vehicle establishing this connection and is seen as racial prejudice, was imported into ethnocentric theories of the market that so often involved the exclusion of developing countries from decision making in their own country. The rational choice turned them into labourers in industry, where they were supervised but never supervisor. That emphasised that the role of self-interest factors of colonial development as a determinant policy that enhances the marginalisation of people in developing countries cannot be left out as one of the influential factors, and hence highlighted the importance of power in these relations.

Therefore, this chapter explores people's views about social structures that lack sustainable development's ability to meet needs in the present and the future in developing countries. It looks at rights and wrongs, and places the blame for the political consequences of polarisation in developing countries on the colonial belief in a superstructure that failed to support the traditional institutions in functioning as a whole. Recent World Trade Organisation periodic reports claim that global trade mitigates the effects of the economic crisis (WTO Director-General Pascal Lamy, during a conference at the United Kingdom Department for International Development on 22 January 2009.).

Increased instability in global markets seems to have interrupted the ability to create economic sustainability, perhaps the starkest reminder that the global economic meltdown is no phantom.

To an extent, for the first time the WTO seems to have acknowledged its realisation that multilateral trading companies have policies and measures that continue to hinder the development of third world countries. The IMF also cited the 'pernicious feedback loop' linking financial markets and the wider economy, reiterating that recovery in the financial sector is a key to wider economic stability. Its report states that growth in developing countries fell by 1 per cent in 2008 and will fall by less than 2 per cent in 2009. This deteriorating outlook is likely to have a ripple effect that will further undermine the growth prospects of a majority of developing countries that depend on the European Union (EU) for their export market. According to the report, these policies include protectionism that leaves most of the developing countries with their exports. It was noted that developing countries' chief exports, such as oil, minerals, agricultural commodities, textiles and clothing as well as tourism, are already experiencing substantial reductions as global demand shrinks (http://uk.f867.yahoo.com/dc/laun ch?patner=bt1&rand=Ig42hmhj6o/03/01/09).

Global trends in international trade and trade policy should ensure that developed countries do not exploit developing countries through protectionism. This is viewed as the objective of a level playing field to provide developing countries with favourable conditions and enable them to reap the benefits of the expansion of trade. The WTO will also ensure the affordability of import and export finance for developing countries. I would add that, if the objective of colonial administrations in developing countries was to create a superstructure, then it was obliged to ensure that all people were protected and secured 'from cradle to grave'. In other words, issues surrounding the superstructure theory have been said to have had a terrible impact on each country and have influenced how people relate to each other; the effect of underdevelopment is directly on the people. The actual criticism of superstructure theory was that its design of unrealistic economic development could neither be serviceable after independence nor provide opportunities for all people in developing countries.

The possibility of achieving economic development in the future hung in the balance, instead reducing the populations of developing countries to entrenched inequalities where young people were pushed onto the streets in a search for unavailable jobs. In effect, the analysis of one of the areas, if not the most dominant, in which racial bias has been clearly perpetuated, represents the development process of countries, societies and humanity as a whole. It is argued that the concept of development must focus on human values, leading to several factors that are necessary for the basic process of development: growth in the output of goods and services; satisfactory progress towards social goals; relative equity in the distribution of the benefits of development; liberating progress and humanisation. In this way, ignoring the importance of a long-term liberating strategy at the early stage of development structuring only focused the development structure to enable the colonisers to exploit the colonies in the long term. Ignoring long-term developmental policies was a clear indication of conspicuous theories and approaches that favoured some people and disadvantaged others.

Peter Uvin specifically draws attention to the fact that for the vast majority of poor developing countries, life is characterised by great 'structural violence' as evidenced by extreme inequality, absence of life chances, social exclusion and deprivation of self-respect (Uvin, P. and Warren, M. A. C., 1994). He argues that the exclusion of equal, ethical values had a negative effect on long-term performance and development policies. The superstructure concept is therefore seen as a result of a myriad of factors, with the overarching element being its structural violence that laid the groundwork for conflict as a result of the pursuit of ideological policies that contained polarised theories of conflict, promoted during the colonial culture rule of violence and ethnocentric theories in colonies. The tangible physical structure of developing countries' economies imposed by colonialism seriously undermined the traditional structures of society, which combined a central authority with a degree of constitutionally defined autonomy for sub central units of government, usually territorial units in the form of decentralised states (Elderly survivors at Gahini Mission interviewed July 1998).

In this respect, there was a mixture of social characteristics in changes in regional provinces, arguing that the past colonial economy meant a loss of the region's autonomous and national sovereignty, which in turn meant the distortion of economic development and the means of production. It is this idea of creating a social structure but limiting its exercise that is particularity distinctive of colonial development interests with a hidden policy of control of the developing country's economy. It is also important to note that other influences were behind much that was happening in developing countries during colonial rule.

A good example is found in Maquet's views, which tend to obscure the real agenda behind colonisation. He raises suspicion about the traditional arrangements, arguing that they served only the Tutsis in dominating the Hutus. He characterises the traditional ritual arrangements as a 'caste system'. The two principal castes referred to are Hutu agriculturalists and Tutsi herders (Maquet, J. J., (1954). Le Système des Relations Sociales dans le Rwanda Ancien. Tervuren: Musée, (Annales du Musée royale du Congo belge, Sciences de l'homme, ethnocide, 1, p.81)

Maquet points out two methods used by Tutsis to exploit Hutus. First, the Tutsis only made up 10 per cent of the population, which enabled the minority to be served by the majority. Secondly, the physical appearance of the Tutsis, with their slender figure and light skin, was used as a sign of superiority over the Hutus, who are of ordinary stature. This clearly illustrates how even scholars have defended the colonial policies and ideology of ethnicity, suggesting that ethnic divisions had existed even before the advent of colonial rule in developing countries (http://www.jha.greatlakes/July 20, 2000) Maquet's assertion was disputed as misleading by respondents from various sources, since before the colonials came to developing countries there were no political conflicts among people. This is, however, argued as overlooking the fact that developing countries had lived together peacefully for centuries (Interviews at Gahini, Kigali and Butare National University August 1998). In other words, it is important to gain insight into the criticisms raised about the nature of colonial development in terms of the national development growth and human development required for political stability, with 'law and order' as its prime concern.

Local criticism of colonial policies, which are partly seen as the source of conflict, embedded a development structure in developing countries that promoted and created racial differences and the use of violence. Racial differences have led to violence and suffering throughout the post-war period, even in developed countries, for example:

- Racial violence and the 1950s urban disorder
- The emergence of the Teddy Boys in the mid-1950s
- The emergence of 'Paki-bashing' in the late 1960s
- The involvement of 'skinhead' gangs and the National Front in the 1970s.

The ideas of social structural functionalism theory offer an explanation that has been highly influential in shaping what Talbot Parsons correctly observed in his theory of structural function encouraged the idea of supremacy between the 1950s and 1970s.

Evidence of racially motivated hate crime and forms of the idea of supremacy meant that the structure of colonial ideological development was associated with a psychological theory of supremacy hidden in the use of biological theory and opening the door to the creation of exploitative, stereotyping development structures (Parsons, T., (1969). Politics and Social Structures, New York: The Free Press. p. 64) Analysis of the history of colonial rule so far indicates that there was a sidelining of developing countries' roles; the process of socio-development was no exception to the racial trend. It seemed rather to be one of the core areas, where the polarised nature of human development was clearly manifested and received much attention. This exclusion was expressed by local interviewees in terms of them being treated as if they had inferior brainpower or a lack of leadership qualities. The use of this biological theory convincingly explains the approach and practice of the colonial phenomenon, as analysed in Berger and Luckmann's theory of constructed reality. In relation to colonial development in former colonial countries, Berger and Luckmann's theory of how reality is constructed, ordered and maintained commits the familiar error of attempting to divorce the concept from the problem of the natural human fear of uncertainty.

If differences in biological or psychological development could be found, it is thought that the influence of the early work of Lombroso (November 6, 1836 to October 19, 1909.), an Italian criminologist who became famous and then infamous for his attempts to find biological differences among people, would provide a lead. Despite Lombroso's specific ideas of biological traits being largely discredited, this did not stop the continuation of the search for biological differences between colonies (http://www.d.umn.edu/~jhamlin1/biological.html/14/7/07; Coleman, Alice (1988). 'Design Disadvantage and Design Improvement; The Criminologist, vol. 12, p.20).

It is argued that the biological differences were either the influence of the nature of rationality or subjectivity embedded in the ethnic distinction theory, which is seen as a combination of both ethnocentric and ideological development exploitation mechanisms as used in colonial days (Lakeland, (1997), Post Modernity: Christian Identity in a Fragmented Age, Minneapolis, Minn.: Fortress, p.12.). This is seen as a theory that was 'conflict making', which is to say that ideally, the period was a convergence of post-colonial and post-modernist programmes in new cultural politics. Bankers in developing countries were led by capitalist interests to generate new theoretical perspectives that challenged developing countries in traditional established institutions. In practical terms, it is argued that this is why the colonial psychology around development interests became the colony's development reality. However, this psychological economy created divisions that seem to have aimed at disparities of group power in the country, evidenced by their lack of naturalisation and neutralisation of the market, which strikingly reveals how the reconstruction of the development system seemed to have had no long-term meaningful purpose for developing countries.

Therefore, a situation analogous to that of the colonial conceptualisation in developing countries is regarded as having been based on the concept of an ethnocentric development structure or superstructure (Lakeland, (1997), Post Modernity: Christian Identity in a Fragmented Age, Minneapolis, Minn.: Fortress, p.12.) Because it operates through ethnocentric theories, the psychological fear that can be traced as being linked with colonial policies was designed to discriminate against developing countries, as they did not accommodate the circumstances of social groups or plans for long-term development in colonies. This is why the colonial development reality construction theory is open to a number of criticisms (http://www.cpnm.org/new/English/articles_news/rootcause_karma.htm).

Norah Lenski et al. argue that people lost the incentive for innovation, knowing that any benefits that resulted from their inventions and discoveries would simply be appropriated by the governing class –

which in this case was the colonial administration (Lenski, G., Nolan, P., and Lenski, J., (1995). Human Societies, an Introduction to Macro Sociology, Seventh Edition, New York: McGrawHill, Inc., p. 186). In particular, a common criticism was aimed at the way the transformation of traditional development structures lacked ethical operating principles for social responsibility and values that took account of social welfare. A positive, pragmatic, structured and functional approach was essential because, as in every society, developing countries had beliefs and systems in operation, in this case based in part on a sense of collective duty known as 'Uburetwa'. Uburetwa was arranged institutionally, mediating social relations, notably in the clan system, which spanned all developing countries.

The system is described by Dalton as follows: 'the bonds of kinship, which structure families, clans and Kings, are often the bonds which organise development activities' (Dalton, G., (Ed.), (1967). Tribal & Peasant Economics, Readings in Economic Anthropology, Texas: Press Sourcebooks in Anthropology, p. 8). Moreover, unlike hunter-gatherer societies, Uburetwa had a well-organised operational system to apply social welfare and private ownership before it was greatly distorted and undermined by the colonial administration. The accurate identification of these developments had wider ramifications. Linden argues from the point of 'the transformation of a complex "feudal" social mobility into a bureaucratic colonial state that hardened social and development differences into rigid class differences and finally resulted in "tribal conflict"' (Linden, Ian, (1997). "The Church and Genocide, Lessons from Rwandese Tragedy", in Baum, Gregory & Wells, Harold (Des), The Reconciliation of peoples, Challenges to the Churches, Maryknoll, NY: Obis Books; Geneva: WCC Publications, pp.41-43). Rene Lemarchand adds that, on the contrary, the image projected by the media of the patterns of exclusion brought to light during and after independence cannot conceal 'deep-seated, ancestral enmities' (Lemarchand, Rene (1994). Managing Transition Anarchies: Rwanda, Burundi, and South Africa in Comparative Perspective, The Journal of Modern African Studies, 32, 4, Cambridge: University Press, p.598). This is true. Tracing the origin of ethnic conflict within the colonial administrative development structure shows the likelihood of conflict being created in the long run in any sort of economy that does not take account of the local view (Ibid.).

is therefore argued that the influence of foreign racial and economic interests created a political climate of violence and harassment. As a process, discourses of race heightened the premature struggle for independence in the 1950s and 1960s. After independence the economic structural models that had been inherited were discovered to be unworkable, and it was during this period when incompetent totalitarian rule was ushered in. Yet the renewal of traditional structures was needed, since their abolition led to a failure to provide a working framework of strategic responsibility for specific roles in the process of development. On the other hand, it is argued that equality of treatment in the colonial administration was necessary to offer opportunities for the emphasis to be placed on rules guaranteeing equality of treatment. The lack of local participation was seen as an infringement of people's rights. Any process that undervalues people and discounts their participation as a fundamental feature of its reality should be treated with profound suspicion.

The analysis of these developments reveals the nature of violence in the past and how it is increasingly embedded in different ways in the modern structural and cultural constraints on groups' interaction (Duly, G., Creating Violence – Free Society: the Case of Rwanda, Journal of Humanitarian Assistance, July 20, 2000, pp.3-11). The incarceration of young people has increased greatly both in Western and developing countries as a result of the increase in unemployment. However, the incarceration of young offenders rather than their rehabilitation seems to have created in Western countries a larger underclass that might depend on welfare for the rest of their lives. It could be replaced by the use of 'New Youth Justice', a process of dejuvenilisation (decriminalisation) where the legal system pays more attention to core assumptions, pre-emptive interventions and non-custodial sentences, Developing countries are pushed further to imprison criminal groups as the only option in a situation where there is no welfare system.

Worldwide statistics on children accommodated in secure units show an increase in those staying longer in incarceration as a form of exclusion. All of these developments reveal how society faces up to the huge implications of cultural shifts in boundaries of inclusion, which are continually shifting under people's feet without their realising. However, in many ways the idea of a culturally diverse economy would go beyond the prevention of political violence into broader co-operation concerns about safety, quality of life and responsibility. Conflict has occurred over how the notion is to be understood and how broad the remit of violence is.

Rose's approach is for offenders to serve their punishment in a form of reparation to the victim and to provide reassurance that the latter's suffering has been acknowledged and taken into account, not simply ignored in the process of discipline that is part of punishment. The belief is often that the purpose of separation in prison is to allow each prisoner to reflect on his or her misdeeds in solicitude, but in the case of younger offenders it instead tends to make them into hard-core criminals because of the influence of other prisoners.

During my prison chaplaincy, I observed that those segregated from others, often as the result of disobedience to prison orders, became more aggressive and prone to violent outbursts, even to the extent of self-harming. This to me was a type of behaviour that was either attention seeking or representative of a rationality crisis, where individuals conclude that there is no reason even for living. It is for this reason that those in the segregation wing always have someone to watch them in case they attempt suicide.

The social function of prison punishment is to discipline and to enforce the purpose of justice, therefore it is inclusive of redress for the victim of the offence and rehabilitation for the perpetrator to realise the serious damage that their action caused. This is not in any way to suggest that a perpetrator should visit the victim in their hospital bed, but rather to rehabilitate the offender through helping them to understand the damage that their offence has caused to society, to their family and to themselves.

There is more than one way of trying to modify offenders' behaviour, where it stems from a lack of education or because discipline was not available at an early stage for those offenders, provided by institutions such as school, prison, hospital, monastery or workhouse. All these institutions provide discipline and restorative punishment aimed at rehabilitation. The reasoning for these programmes was developed by cognitive psychologist Robert Ross, based on research carried out in a Canadian prison. The programmes were also based on Farrington's theory of 'delinquencies, the cognitive (thinking skills) in which they were deficient, in the expectation that this would lead to a decrease in their offending' (Farrington 1996).

Such rehabilitation programmes were widely used, especially in UK prison establishments by youth offending teams (YOTs), to help restore younger offenders to being law-abiding citizens. The purpose of this rehabilitation is seen as offering a chance to provide the kind of education and discipline that was lacking for these individuals in their family, schools and community. From the restorative point of view to restore relationships is the key emphasis, which is another way of investing in rehabilitation and reintegrating into society those who have committed minor offences.

The programme of discipline has to be established with a good communication system. For it to be restorative the detention centre managers must first supply the ingredients lacking in the original impaired decision making of each offender so that they act as expected by society. It is essential to have an immediate response where such provision is compatible with public safety; it seems to have a number of powerful advantages over custody. The process must be clearly explained to the offender. It should be emphasised that the offenders are at odds with the whole ethos of living as responsible citizens. All information about the rehabilitation programme is made available to offenders. Particular trouble spots must be identified and tackled. A coherent standard of discipline must be explained and applied throughout each session, so that everyone clearly understands what is acceptable and what is unacceptable behaviour.

Rose went further to pose two questions of victims, offered to show how their grievances are often overlooked or ignored and suggested how they can be addressed. The approach suggested is actuarial justice, addressing the victim's grievances. What is proposed as the role of risk management (containing) is denying individuals the choice of responsibility for any decision or action. In addition, it makes it possible for those involved to design messages that are in context and specific, which eventfully will help to modify behaviour and encourage the development of desirable communal habits. This is how rehabilitation can make a profound contribution in an individual's life, playing a positive role in building human capacity to move on from past failings.

There will be a rehabilitation panel, whose function will be to agree a contract with the offender for a programme of behaviour for a specific period. Feely and Simon explain the clear emphasis on the constructive aspects of the programme by comparing actuarial justice and incarceration. Rather than empowering offenders through the rehabilitation panel, the programmes work to change the perpetrators and include teaching them how to control themselves. The panel approach to criminal justice brought with it a flurry of research, which found significant behaviour change in offenders. The rehabilitation programme takes a 'what works' approach to intervention models, including the widely used cognitive behavioural therapy models, and explores the theories of crime that have informed their development.

The programme is to be guided by three principles of 'restorative justice': financial or other reparation to the victim, reintegration into the community, and taking responsibility for the consequences of offending behaviour. Thus, in addition to specific reparations, the programme may require the offender to carry out community service, attend school or a workplace, accept a curfew at specified times, participate in activities involving education, training or rehabilitation from drug or alcohol abuse, report at specified time and places and stay away from particular places or people.

A considerable amount of research has been carried out, both in the UK and in America, which demonstrate evidence of 'what works' in this specific area. Thus, in addition to specific reparations, providing training in controlling aggression and to provide skills eventually leads to employment. Since most offenders live in poverty, have been displaced by political conflicts or have run away as children from domestic violence, the best discipline is to transform them into useful and good citizens through providing them with skills.

There is a moral obligation for both the national and the international community to help such people and at least to offer them the minimum standard of education recommended by the United Nations. The United Nations Convention, 1990, Article 28 states that all countries should prepare children to lead a responsible life in society in the spirit of understanding, peace, tolerance, equality of sexes, respect of human rights and friendship among all people, ethnic, national and religious groups and persons of indigenous origin (United Nations

Charter, 1990). A restorative approach is seen as more appropriate, especially in developing countries where crime is committed out of a need to survive.

All human beings are supposed to be born free and equal in dignity and rights. Because by nature human species are endowed with reason and conscience and should act towards one another in a spirit of common destiny, it is therefore argued that the practice of diversity should consider cultural development within a wider, global context. In particular, this draws on the conflict between developed and developing countries over institutional control and trade markets. Alternative discourses reveal the meaning and limitations of developing countries' safety in the developmental context. As there are no simple explanations, research indicates that certain types of violence have their roots in various internal and external influences; for example, they are internal when a husband keeps his wife in the subordinate role that women have traditionally held in private and public life in many societies.

The United Nations charter reaffirms faith in fundamental human rights, in the dignity and worth of the human person and in the equal rights of men and women. It is determined to promote social progress and better standards of life. It also shows how various societies have organised themselves to respond in different ways, such as a voluntary organisation like Amnesty International that polices violations of human rights globally. In theory and practice the charter was a call for a common standard of achievement for all peoples and all nations, every individual and every organ of society, keeping this principle constantly in mind, and that each state should teach its citizens to promote respect for the declaration. It describes violence against civilians, or women in the case of domestic violence, as 'a manifestation of historically unequal power relationships between men and women'. Although its principle was mutual non-interference in the internal affairs of states, in practice gross breaches of rights have led to UN and NATO intervention.

During my work as a prison chaplain there were offenders who would confess that they were force to committee a crime rather than being on the streets; in other words, they wanted to get off the streets and preferred to be incarcerated, since trying to live on the outside without any source of legal income is more costly and dangerous than being in prison. Therefore, rehabilitation which offers skills is better than a government's preference for excluding offenders or managing crime rather than dealing with the causes of crime (Feely & Simon, 1992). Foucault and Cohen were highly influential in shaping what Hudson described as the 'social control' perspective (Hudson, 2002). O'Malley and Rose both neatly outlined how Hudson's infamous social control theory of 'actuarial justice' was reflective and constructive of a more profound decline in a collective willingness to share exposure to collective risks (O'Malley 1992; Rose 1996).

In general, Western countries apply penal policies, especially in the US where punishment is weighed heavily in favour of incarceration, to the detriment of forms of rehabilitation that offer hope in the long run after punishment.

Foucault famously noted that 'knowledge is power' and that changing ways of thinking offers a new vision of society. He explained that self-harm and societies are closely bound up with changing the offender's social perspective and rationality of social control (Foucault, M., 1977:17-23). This all suggests that society's effort should be put into accountability programmes for offenders to assist prisons or detention centres in developing discipline and enhancing the offender's ability to be accountable to societal expectations and to act responsibly. The rehabilitation programme as social goal provides information sharing and evaluation of crime-prevention efforts. The system assesses individual offenders on the basis of their location, region and coordinated effort while serving the punishment and after punishment, to monitor the possibility of reoffending before it happens.

The idea of rehabilitation and restoration must go hand in hand to promote discipline by use of a model that promotes justice and human rights and nurtures routine aspects of behaviour and the concept of change through the use of an inclusive model, not excluding offenders and alienating or incarcerating them so that they continue as dysfunctional individuals, which eventually leads them in violent behaviour. The idea of discipline is not necessarily control of activities, but rather monitoring routine behaviour and elaboration of acceptable behaviour or conducts. On the other hand, the priority of an offender's punishment should be a process of rehabilitation in the form of social reform rather than incarceration.

Foucault's historical analysis of the disciplinary society is relevant here, where he identified some important and relevant trends in the contemporary state of social change, particularly with regard of the role of the state. For instance, Godden's analysis of late modernity suggests that the rapid changes intensified and accelerated through communities, disarming and disempowering institutions such as families, religions, community culture, communal shared values and educational institutions, removing the social restraints that are at the heart of moulding and nurturing the positive human relations on which society depends for interaction (Gidden 1990;1991). In fact, the types of violence that prevail in the world are a by-product of the societies we have created, as we will see later.

The values of self-interest seem to have triumphed over the social collective values of caring for one another. Once communities are separated by high-rise buildings and individuals become dislocated and isolated in concrete buildings where they are no longer, concern for the community dissipates. It is arguable that the trend today is for care to be left to the professionals: teachers, police, social workers, doctors, churches and probation officers. While the growing culture of violence is evidence of humans becoming irresponsible and losing a sense of care for one another, this is the society that we have created in our generation in the name of discriminatory beliefs or ideological theories.

Cohen and Innes went further to argue a number of other causes of violence, such as the lack of social structures and the way that authorities control society by introducing repressive measures and policies that push individuals to seek sanctuary elsewhere. Therefore, through understanding society and the development of structural functioning (productive) relations and developments in the world related to the above factors, we can discount the claims of a lack of civilisation or of having nothing to do with biological criminality, as we shall see later. Today all the available evidences shows that the crime rate is increasing in both poor and rich countries, where modernity is also seen as contributing to either domestic violence or crimes of various types such as domestic, robbery and political conflicts. These are all related to trivialising violence in films as entertainment, which will be assessed in this chapter to highlight its effect on the younger generation and discuss the psychological impact of it in relation to the control of violence.

It is not my purpose to argue that the exclusion of the historical evidence of political conflicts in developing countries would fill the chasm between normal and abnormal conditions. But the admission of much such evidence of societal structures generates a situation in which infringements of social codes constitute abnormality; that is to say, an expected reaction out of frustration and a response of violence. Its exclusion would go some way towards the creation of abnormal conditions in the sense of what is socially expected in society, which may be interpreted in different ways, but is seen as the normal reaction of people under abnormal conditions. There is the question of the way violence is committed: it may be political, state sanctioned in the form of punishment or domestic.

Therefore, it is flawed and even wrong to assume that the conflict in developing countries has to do with a lack of civilisation, whether it is committed by the use of machetes or guns. Violence robs people of their lives and their right to existence. The glamorisation of violence in the form of advertisements for weaponry that appear on television or in a form of non-regulated violent entertainment is regarded by some people as rather irresponsibly promoting the use of violence. Becoming critically aware of the content of advertising and its potential impact on human and natural systems is, of course, just one way of promoting violence. The negative discourse that is equally important in the context of the media's added influence is the indirect impact of advertising and how a certain category of media creates a buying mood among Third World countries' dictators in order to sell deadly weapons to them.

I will further argue that politicians in developing countries need to wake up to the fact that the prominence given to the role of violence as a means of accumulating wealth is barbaric, primitive and degrading. It only highlights the primitive old ways and does not make a positive, idealistic response to the crisis of violence caused by inept policies. Furthermore, the global media have invaded millions of homes and are watched daily on which violence is regarded as entertainment and yet they influence families and nations where the most vulnerable are intoxicated with bad influences. Advertising is, of course, embedded within the global economic discourse, and awareness of this is essential for politicians, since Western dominant foreign policies are frequently based on economic interests.

This, then, is the most obvious example of the prevalent increase of violence in developing countries. We need to gain awareness of the economic forces that frame the violent cultural and creative forces from developed industries, which see economic growth (whatever the source) as something that perpetuates a misperception of arbitrary arbitrariness, so that it comes to be seen as transparently and morally reflecting economic and democratic realities rather than constructing or fixing permanent conflict in many ways in developing countries. It is therefore argued that through analysis of what is happening globally, leaders in developing countries become aware of some of the parameters of the world they live in, parameters that could provide a reality for evaluating good governance and be turned into action when these leaders resist the discourse that promotes the use of arms and human damage, preferring the use of negotiation to purchasing unnecessary weapons, which do not provide a lasting solution to grievances.

Domestic violence can also be attributed to watching too many horror movies, which can be dangerous to some individuals. Evidence from criminological investigations reveals that in most cases this does have an influence on young people, especially the disadvantaged, and can create a sense of personal inadequacy in areas such as interaction, shyness and a perception of inner failure in the face of challenging situations. It is this very situation that highlights the intersection of race and gender in criminal justice policies and practice.

Being aware of the background to and place of gender of the workings of the criminal justice system is a necessary response to pressing social problems and a punitive system guaranteed to exclude those who come into contact with it as 'crime perpetrators', as shown in the specific experience of minority ethnic females in their encounters with criminal justice institutions (Carlen, P., (1998). Women, Crime and Poverty. Milton Keynes: Open University Press). The media profile all sorts of violence, highlighting the very real issues faced by women and children in these situations. For instance, in developing countries the lack of economic resources dangerously affects people's ability to work and has led to an increase in domestic violence; it is retarding the development of these countries in situations where there is no financial assistance.

Worldwide evidence reveals the increasing occurrence of violent crimes and a culture of moral deviance. Domestic violence can include verbal abuse and the silent method, where a partner may provide everything to the spouse as required, but cuts off communication. Among other violent crimes include incidents where husbands or wives burn their partners with hot cooking oil. Other incidents that have been witnessed in recent years are violence from farmers after poor harvests of agricultural produce, even children killing their own fathers when the latter fail to maintain their families and to provide financial assistance to children for school fees and instead waste money on alcohol and prostitutes; co-wives in polygamous marriages killing each other; men killing their former wives or defiling and raping underage children and women, which are all blamed on domestic violence. It is also notable that children either become victims of infanticide or parents send their daughters into commercial sex as a means of earning a living, which has led to increase in abortion.

In addition to this, from the scientific point of view Mennell argues that there are broad categories of social relations, which are both constructed around us and in turn shape and reshape human reactions. This ability derives from the development of anatomical and neurological features that enable people to relate to their situation and their place within it (Mennell, 1974:253).

For instance, watching violent films has been shown to turn some people into serial killers, as a result of the influence of all sorts of criminal imaginings directly associated with the critical faculty that develops in the upper brain. The way in which the term 'serial killer' came into existence is interesting. During the mid-1970s, the FBI agent Robert K. Ressler coined this phrase after serial movies. As Lippit argues, 'Like each episode of a serial movie, the completion of each serial murder lays the foundation for the next act which in turn precipitates future acts, leaving the serial subject always wanting more, always hungry, addicted (http://serendp.brynmawr.edu/bb/neuro/neuro04/web2/.cdeputy. html ; Lippit, Akira Mizuta. "The infinite series: fathers, cannibals, chemists..." Criticism. Summer 1996: 1-18, A Good Article).'

One other fact that it is important for modern society to recognise is that the myth of the home is a thing of the past, since the technological invention of televisions, DVDs and computer games has replaced family conversations where people sat and worked out any issues concerning family affairs; the loss of these often leads to an increase in tension. Whereas in the past society relied on family, church or religious institutions and community values as restraints in social control, modernity has dismissed these institutions, which are regarded by society, especially Western society, as irrelevant; instead, society has shifted its trust to the presence of the police, courts and other agencies of crime control.

Social scientists recognise that, to a greater or lesser extent, over the past 50 years all societies have gone through tremendous social changes. In most if not all circumstances solutions lie in the medium- to longer-term issues of tackling inequalities, differentiation, deprivation and inconsistencies in foreign policies, which need to be reviewed to prevent extremism. Militant activism is an issue that varies in a systematic way over time and from community to community.

Different eras have been identified, such as post-modernity, hyper-modernity, high modernity and late modernity. For instance, Gidden's analysis shows that in late modernity neighbourhoods drastically changed, in that the structures of tolerance and intolerance began to be reversed (Giddens, 1991). Debate on contemporary society described by Cohen shows that, although the changes are motivated by good intentions on the part of the reformers, their ironic and unintended consequences were to develop new forms of control. People become more likely to be less trusting and more fearful as a resulting of the weakening of communities' social glue, the previous resources that people employed to resolve domestic issues, recover from a stressful day or celebrate a successful day together as a family and focus on the issues that mattered (Cohen, 1958:38). Diversity became tolerated and people became disengaged from each another; differences in lifestyle were tolerated while difficulties became less and less tolerable.

The invention and reinvention of community centre cultures in Western countries has been a site of continual negation and struggle within the disengaged cultural boundaries of society's cultural structures. At the same time, the persistence of a quest for social justice is gathering worldwide momentum in a continuing struggle against politically dominant forces. Also new cultures have been brought about by the technological revolution in developed societies, which continues to inform the shifting forwards and backwards of contemporary social structures today.

Society must be prepared to respond to the huge implications of the imbalance that was created in past developmental structures, which are the source of conflict in the modern development group motivation hypothesis, since intra-state wars mainly consist of fighting between groups, and group motives, resentments and ambitions provide the motivation for war (Cfr. Frances.stewart@queen-elizabeth-house. oxford.ac.uk). Resentments inspired by group differences, termed horizontal inequalities, are a major cause of war. A. Swain argued that group inequality and group differences have many dimensions: economic, political and social. Nafziger, Stewart and Vayrynen added that the growing scarcity of water or gracing space may provoke conflict (Swain A. Water scarcity as a source of crises. In: Nafziger EW, Stewart F, Vayrynen R, eds. War, hunger and displacement: the origin of humanitarian emergencies. Oxford: Oxford University Press, 2000:179-205.). There is consistent evidence of sharp horizontal inequalities between groups in conflict (Nafziger EW, Stewart F, Vayrynen R, eds. War, hunger and displacement: the origin of humanitarian emergencies. Oxford: Oxford University Press, 2000). Furthermore, Gurr observed that, although systematic cross-country evidence is rare, one study classified 233 politicised communal groups in 93 countries according to political, economic and ecological differences and found that most groups suffering horizontal inequalities had taken some action to assert group interests, ranging from non-violent protest to rebellion (Gurr TR. Minorities at risk: a global view of ethnopolitical conflicts. Washington DC: Institute of Peace Press, 1993).

Although the cultural boundaries of unity are ever controlled and stuck in the conflict, the profound and noticeable factor of control has pivoted around foreign influence, which can be traced in the diverse policies that have led to this wide crisis. In order to develop a picture of the patterns of wider activities that seem to have created the present state of violence, this book attempts to provide the historical background by looking at the use of repressive policies in colonial rule related to superiority beliefs and theories. We have assessed the controversial term racism and how ethnocentric theory describes the use of ideological rule introduced during the colonial period, which has haunted former colonies for many years and hampered the ideal objectives of providing all countries with equal access to a common market, wealth and development, and the sanctioned use of violence in the form of punishment. We now need to address the nature of wider issues that led young people from deprived societies to radical militant belief; to seek to explain the cause of civil conflict in developing countries; and to consider what is needed to make the cost of living there less expensive.

Chapter five

The social background of violence

Why violence is on increase

This chapter looks at how violence has gradually increased in various ways. It starts in homes and violence as a habit grows bigger, to the extent that it ceases to be domestic and eventually spills over into the public realm, where as a result it causes pain and suffering to others and the whole of society suffers consequentially. Many people in developing countries are subjected to terrifying experiences of violence. Most of these are women, elderly, disabled and children, who are victims of violence and torture by their lovers, husbands, fiancées, fathers or mothers and neighbours. Amidst all this, you can't help but ask whether the human rights convention is too northern/Western in its social and cultural protection, or whether it reflects a process of excessive compromise. Are its terms too general to be of any use in practical terms? That only confirms the critical voices so often heard saying that Western countries have, as usual, raised their concerns only and only where it concerns their interests.

In these chapter, I will consider the main issues arising out of the ratification of the UN convention to assess whether it is a response to violence as a means of liberation or not. The discussion will also consider the significance of the response to ideas of diversity in developmental strategic programmes. To do so I have decided to explore the spaces that human beings occupy in social cultural worlds and the interactions that humans have with each other. Central to this interaction is an exploration of the ways in which rich societies pin down less fortunate societies in a cross-examination of how different members of the human race construct a range of identities for themselves and for others in terms of development interest.

The emphasis is to highlight differences of causation of violence, either through the media as a source, religious beliefs, culture, rituals or politics used to escalate it. For instance, ritual closely connected with birth, ritual naming, initiation into adulthood, marriage, death and solidarity or focused on continuing relations with ancestors can be seen as harmless. This raises issues relating to creation. Secondly, social forces have an impact; the discussion will concentrate on demonstrating the effects on both the domestic and the wider use of violence to show how families must put emphasis in the home on nurturing young family members.

Conventional norms and family values need to be introduced, as well as how to use an interactive standard approach to providing young people with skills that they can learn from, such as how to listen to others, self-control under pressure or challenge, tolerance, patience, and how to communicate effectively. In this way the use of violence can be avoided or addressed at an early stage of a child's growth. The discussion will assess the effects of violence on children, mothers and society at large.

Another critical emphasis is to be found in the mechanism of the trade market, where there is no easy or straightforward answer to the long-term dominance of external political development, whereas the inappropriate choice of a colonial political ideology in development policies has continued to be controlled by developing countries as a consequence of a number of factors, including differences in the productivity and development strength of individual economies participating in an integrated market. However, it is necessary for Western countries to realise that development has become a 'power game', and that for developing countries to become involved in the 'power game' they have to walk a tightrope between Western countries' policies and retaining the interests of local people. When there are development constraints in any society it is harder to move forward in constructive development.

Therefore, it is necessary to analyse the social ethics of the world market and foreign policies in practical development underpinning of the use of violence, which contributes to the creation of radical beliefs. A creative struggle against poverty in line with development liberates the poor and prevents them suffering from frustration and powerlessness. The liberation theory of the poor is the most potent tool and is seen as the cause of a necessity in developing countries to fight for freedom from poverty as a positive response to political violence.

Based on these premises, Western countries are perceived as being in control of what happens in developing countries, therefore their policies are discussed to suggest an alternative response that will allow developing countries to solve their problems. A determined sceptic might acknowledge that help from the West simply maintains its control, therefore the development system and all that it includes has a very limited possibility of succeeding, because, critically, the development system cannot function effectively without access to the world market.

The problem of the role of foreign economic interests in sales of arms and in investments unhelpful to local economy, despite its denial by industrial countries, has been submerged in the subsequent use of violence in most developing countries that refuse to dance to the tune of political dictatorship. The resulting political conflicts and constant wars have become a cultural norm in developing countries (former colonies) and are frighteningly on the increase. The situation of foreign interference is conceived of in this way: the situation induces developing countries to use violence in the interests of dictatorship, which hinders national development; where the local leadership does not agree with the opposition they either starve them out or create an emergency situation, which leads to political conflicts and wars.

The most depressing issue is how human lives have become a political tool to ensure that certain factions remain in power. For instance, the denial of humanitarian assistance and medical treatment in Zimbabwe is beyond imaginable; to deny citizens their human right to existence is a gross injustice for the world community is accountable in its failure to act and reach dying people, as well as aid agencies' inability to set up an organisational structure in the capital, Harare. 'The people of Zimbabwe voted for a better future. It is our duty to support that aspiration,' said Prime Minister Brown, one day after US Secretary of State Condoleezza Rice commented,' the outbreak is the latest sign that Mugabe's rule over the country must end. It's well past time for Robert Mugabe to leave. I think that's now obvious' (World News CNN.com/22/11/08).

I wish to critically analyse this worldwide problem, as a record for the next generation to see the level of the mess this generation has created. It is difficult to get away from the common-sense view that the wrong decisions have been made. I feel that my role as an ordained priest and qualified social scientist it to be an agent of holistic changing societies and to suggest an end to waging war on humanity. I wish to agree with former President Jimmy Carter's comments that President Obama's decision to close Guantánamo Bay detention centre and end US-sponsored torture will be a strong signal of its commitment to universal human rights (Ibid.)

The initial source of violence can be divided into two categories: family domestic violence and violence promoted through the film industry, which is seen as a source of influence on younger people. John H. Richardson quotes Professor Sylvère Lotringer, who taught a class on death and who once told me that the cheap horror movies I loved in those days (from Halloween to The Evil Dead) were 'an inoculation' against violence in society (Richardson, John, H., bluegrassfilmsociety. blogspot.com/2008/12/john-h-richardson-my-history-of.html) Killers have been shown to internalise the verbal abuse that they receive from members of their family and apply it to their victims; for example Robert Simon referred to his victims as worthless little queers and punks (http://serendp.brynmawr.edu/bb/neuro/neuro04/web2/.cdeputy. html ; Simon, Robert. "Serial Killers, Evil, and Us." National Forum. Fall 2000: 1-12, A Good Article) Income inequalities harm well-being, not just of the poor but among a large majority of the population, and add to rates of violence, physical and mental illness and numerous social problems. Experiences of terrifying violence evoke sadness and make one wonder how human being can be more inhumane than wild beasts. The meanings expressed in such acts can be understood by examining the context of domination and manipulation.

It is on these grounds that religious wisdom opposes the exploitation of violence for entertainment, rejecting the claim that it is a form of theatre. In a variety of ways human beings have used and still use other human beings to perform good and bad acts in the same way that they use domestic animals to perform different tasks, such as hunting or entertainment. But we should not be responsible for portraying intolerance as normal, and the worst situation is where human beings are used like bullfighters; wars in developing countries are often judged in a similar context.

The whole argument against violence concerns the manipulation of social meaning expressed in its performance. It can be understood by examining how the use of violence is perhaps fundamental in establishing anthropomorphism, which is, in this context, the attribution of supposedly human qualities to the motive for a person to act. This is perhaps realism expressed in its most complex way, for international relationships create doubts, frustration and the envious passion of the mob for selfish or political forces to treat another human being so inhumanely.

Ethnocentric theories and colonial ideologies emphasised the role of self-interest in detrimental acts of violence and in political policies. Hence the importance of economic power tells us about human societies and a drive for psychological liberation seems to have emerged out of these developments. Another important development is to recognise that the new violent culture does not represent oppressed societies in a natural way but as a charismatic individual's response to oppressed societies -they give a cultural or religious meaning to the cause of action. Many developing societies have come to be regarded as oppressed societies and various organisations have set about arguing for, and fighting for, a change in this status.

Therefore, this chapter explores the moral concerns surrounding the ideas of radical organisations that desire to make an impact on movements dedicated to liberation. It is important to recognise here how elements of religious faith and social justice are intertwined in the aspects of radical liberation.

The struggle for liberation is part of the culture of development and must be understood as interlinked in the sociology and religiosity of radical martyrdom. It definitely makes sense to commit one's life to a cause and incorporate it into one's cosmology, beliefs, practices and acts, associated with gods, spirits and other supernatural beings. However, in recent decades development issues have increased the cultural integration of the representation of religious and social justice and engaged the attention, emotions and thoughts of a wider public, which can be interpreted as a reaction to an awkward situation through the medium of the use of violence.

The increase in violence calls for united action from world leaders to respond effectively to the changing external environment. I get information from the very people who are subject to such misery, the 'down-trodden'. Fresh evidence in developing countries and continual reports in the media reveal that the use of violence tends to be portrayed as applyinhg exclusively to the countries of the South. In one country, Rwanda, there is alarming evidence of attacks against women, including rape, defilement and corporal punishment as well as murder by their husbands. One chilling report revealed that 259 wives were murdered by their husbands in three years. During the same period, over 2000 cases of rape were reported to the police and there were almost 10,000 cases of defilement of children below the age of 18. However, the report did not show statistics concerning gender-based violence against husbands by wives. Sexual harassment is much more widespread and is a major concern in many developing countries; sexual harassment at the workplaces is common (Jeremy Okungui, Africa needs a standby army to deal with her conflicts, 4 East African perspective, Thursday, 13th November/2008). Whether it is domestic violence, state-sanctioned violence in the form of capital punishment, street violence committed in London or New York, or the wider political violence committed in the deserts of the Middle East, the mountains of Afghanistan or the forests of the Congo – these are all violent expressions against some sort of imbalance in development.

More than 80% of the world's population live in countries where there are wide income differentiations compared to Western countries. The top 20% of the richest countries control the resources of the poorest 40% of countries. According to United Nations reports, between 27% and 28% of all children in developing countries are estimated to be undernourished and underweight due to poor feeding and lack of water. The economic evidence indicates that the bulk of the deficit is either in South Asia or on the African continent. Some 1.1 billion people in developing countries live in conditions of poverty without even the basic necessities of life, with one in three living on less than 50 pence a day. Women are forced to collect water over long distances, just in order to survive (Ibid.).

Ironically, there are various misleading superficial explanations for why there are so many political conflicts in developing countries, often attributed to these countries not embracing development and lacking so-called civilisation. Others have attributed the failure of development to black people's laziness. These assumptions about the reality of development not only fail to take into account the role of trade market control, including monetary policies, exchange rates, inflation, capital, employment and labour. All these methods of control are argued as actually colluding with the behaviour and beliefs of industrial economic actors in the perpetuation of the theory or myth of civilisation and biological differences.

In order to develop the argument that perpetuates the myth of civilisation, it is important to note that this is not an accurate claim, as a closer examination reveals that social changes in the past were based on colonialism, as the colonising powers often claimed to be on a civilising mission that would grant independence to colonial peoples 'when they were ready for it'. This became increasingly unacceptable and was often regarded as domination and exploitation of Third World countries. One way of illustrating this argument is by using John M. Rothgeb's research, which examined the relationship between direct foreign investment and political protest in developing countries. A cross-national design was employed to investigate how investments in manufacturing and mining interacted with a society's historical relationship to the world system, its contemporary relationship to the world system, its economic structures, and its rate of social change to affect the population (http://cat.inist.fr/?aModele=afficheN&cpsid=13 841100/5/1/09).

The results of this research showed that manufacturing investments in new states and from former colonial overlords are associated with lower levels of protest, while mining investments from a single foreign national source and in societies with high income inequalities and a strong local capital structure are related to more protests. Large manufacturing and mining investments are associated with higher levels of political conflict than neo-colonialism revisionism would imply (Ibid.).

Unfortunately for the so-called independent population, however, the change of attitude was not accompanied by much willingness to realise that these policies were instruments of long-term exploitation. Dimensions of past and present foreign policies lead to the considerable danger that even the use of civilisation may be not only limited but negatively misleading, because in their assumptions about the lack of development in these countries, commentators place the cause of failure on the nature of people whose biological genes lead to underachievement. This as untrue, and instead it is argued that the economies of rich and largely Western industrial countries, including Japan, have restrictions that deny developing countries access to the open trade market, and that the use of tariffs in foreign policies is an obstacle targeted at poor countries as consumers rather than producers.

If one examines further such arrangements, there are several factors that prevent developing countries from developing, which mostly consist in the economic dominance of Western countries. Clive Crook argues that the answer from orthodox economics is that trade allows countries to exploit their comparative advantage. Trade enables a country to consume a mix of goods that is different from the mix it produces, with prices in world markets acting as the mediator between the two. It is argued that free trade does more than bring about the right mix of products. It also eliminates the inefficiencies in production caused by protectionism. On the other hand, policy protection may make some domestic producers monopolists or near monopolists, thus introducing an inefficiency directly (because monopolists exploit their market strength by producing less and charging more) and indirectly (because, lacking competition, they have no incentive to keep costs low) (Clive Crook, (1992). Article, Third World Economic Development).

To exemplify the use of violence and endless civil wars by the promotion of foreign policies is simply an excuse for claims to support so-called elected leadership and parliamentary democracy, which is always bypassed by the partisan nature of dictatorship. A clear indication of this is that the end of the Cold War and the collapse of communism accelerated the pace of change. Furthermore, it was recognisable that after Cold War the possibility of a new economic order was at the top of the agenda. A closer examination of political developments after the end of the Cold War and the death of communism reveals that what has been happening in the last 50 years has been extremely eventful, not just for industrialised countries but also for developing countries, and especially for their economies.

The use of violence by developing countries' leadership is a political tactic used to keep dictators in power. Political conflict is partly a consequence that characterises the late world order and globalised violence. In the 1990s, for the wealthiest industrialised countries, separation and a clear division emerged in their ability to change and the capability in developing countries. The seemingly inexorable tide of socialism went into rapid reverse and foreign policies developed into political conflicts. It is this mechanism that gives the industrialised countries the ability to define the way poor countries must play the game without the ability inevitably to challenge the past, and the role of current foreign policies has exacerbated the climate of conflict.

It is evident that there were a variety of permutations in the development crisis from the 1970s, when the technological revolution in industrial Western countries brought home the realisation that the old industry model of production was inefficient for competition, and that the continuance of incompetence could lessen the dominance of developing nations. The moral panic in the West was a period of industrial revolution, while others have described this period as capitalism in crisis; racist groups have attributed the cause of the increase in mugging and street violence, which at this period had become endemic in big cities, to black culture.

Racial theory needs to be considered in order to ascertain whether or not the racialisation of mugging is justified. The technological revolution had a far-reaching impact on general social changes that had not been envisaged by policy makers. Their overall effect in society was greatly than had been realised: during this period industrial countries restructured their industry, altered concepts of gender and family, encountered changes in ecology, a growth in media, a rising crime rate and social mobility. All of these in one way or another contributed to an increase of violence, although they could have been contained and hopefully channelled to some good purpose. This has since remained a notable subject of concern in the media, and in political and official discourses on street crime. The concerns draw heavily on criminological debates that accompanied the 'mugging' phenomenon of the 1970s.

Effects of social change

The theoretical literature underpinning the Western side of these changes and the process provides an insight into emerging arrangements evolving from ideological foreign policies in the world today. The point of emphasis here is how the culture of globalisation makes it easy and quick to get information into homes. For example, a UK survey of tobacco use in secondary schools carried out in 2004 jointly by the Ministry for Health and the Ministry for Education, with the support of the World Health Organisation (WHO), indicated that 24 per cent of students in secondary school smoke and consume alcohol.

According to the latest findings in developing countries, youngsters are like their peers in Western countries; the effects on people in developing countries may be not necessarily be on the same level but occur in different ways.

A particular concern is that most of these youngsters have no legal source of income and as a result of being addicted they are forced into illegal behaviour in order to feed their habit. Given that what happens in one place soon becomes a global issue, appropriate social policies are required. Crime prevention and thinking have become dominant and widely practised in contemporary policies (alongside order strategies of criminal justice).

Control in the contemporary legislative response is highly racialised. Reflecting on history illustrates how the objective of reducing offenders' ability to reoffend is to some extent illustrative of community values. On the other hand, the current restraints have ceased to act as restraints in criminal control or managing dangerous or risky populations, the underclass or 'socially excluded'. This journey requires first an examination of the nature and extent of racially motivated hate crime in post-war black and Asian immigration in the West. Secondly, it is argued that taking a critical look at previous and recent policies enables us to realise how these methods have been abused by those in power, especially under the rule of dictatorship, and used to silence the opponents in several parts of the world.

In Western countries some of the most profound effects of crime prevention lie in the key role played by control policies, which pivot around political ideological policies and to extent racial theories. This has been the influence of changes in incarceration towards segregation and differentiation, which are produced by and productive of neo-liberal strategies and risk avoidance (Davis, M. (1990). City of quartz: excavating the future of Los Angels. London. Pimlico, Chapter 4). Central to this argument is not simply the question of being critical but the identification of most exclusion theories behind the lack of development in developing countries. A social or political crisis is so often the source of violence, including ideas of defensible space or offence-based theories such as political rational choice theory. In this case, such routine preventive activities and communitarian and other ideas are aimed at developing techniques of informal social control associated with social crime prevention.

The analysis of incarceration theory highlights the way in which punishment is applied in practice, which critics argue as having undermined early societal cultural restraints and psychological understandings of the relationships between individuals and social community arrangements. Levi-Strauss referred to the magic of such anthropophagic societies to take individuals 'possessing dangerous powers' to neutralise them, 'even turning them to advantage'(Levi-Strauss 1992:388).

This chapter explores the implications of these changes and the concept of exclusion on both a local and wider scale for our understanding of both society and violence, and considers whether these trends are likely to continue or whether there will be moves towards a more radical and diverse notion of social inclusion. Scholars like Garland, Young and Rose have gone further to explain that it is to do with modernity. Society has gone through several changes such as post-structuralism that dispersed power from traditional structures of social control for governance in a process of 'late modernity' (Young 1999, Garland 2000, 2001, Rose 2000). However, in the absence of previous community structures, it is arguable that when these formal community mechanisms cease to exist, individuals drift into deviant anti-social behaviour as a response to social necessities and development needs, seen as accumulating from the pressures arising from society's natural forces (Cohen 1985, Innes 2003). Another important consideration is how the role of race as it affects criminal justice policies and practices has over the years attracted significant interest within and outside academic circles. Another key significant development has been recent legislations and the structure of the Western youth justice system, particularly in terms of recent attempts to inculcate the techniques of restorative justice through youth offender's panels.

More broadly, there is a need to consider whether there is a fundamental difference in the behaviour of young people that would warrant the extension of social control and whether the system for young people is up to the task of talking about problem behaviour. In reference to contemporary legislation, young people's criminalisation or incarceration varies, characterised by numbers of arrests and prison statistics of young people. Conflicting criminological theories that attempt to explain the disproportionate presence of black people in prisons in the northern hemisphere see it as a reflection of the notion of social legitimacy and the effectiveness of previous and contemporary policies in the justice system. (Briton, N. (2000). 'Race and Policing: A Study of Policing Custody', British Journal of Criminology, 40:639-658.).

This refers to Waquant's observation that 'astronomical overrepresentation of blacks in houses of penal confinement and the increasingly tight meshing of the hyper ghetto with the carceeral system suggests that, owing to America's adoption of mass incarceration as a queer social policy designed to deal with the poor cheaply and isolate them, which is in a way seen as another form of modern segregation of the poor and to contain the dishonoured, lower-class African-Americans who now dwell, not in society with prisons as their white compatriots do, but in the first genuine prison society of history (Waquant, L., (2001). 'Deadly Symbiosis: when ghetto and prison meet and mesh' in Garland, D. (ed.). Mass imprisonment: social causes and consequences. London. Sage Publications).

How adequate the incarceration system is in dealing with crime and the behaviour change of these large numbers of young people, therefore, is a question of whether the new techniques of youth justice divert young people from the criminal justice system, or whether the escalating use of legal regulation targets and emphasis on disorder and incivility simply leads to criminalisation and incarceration as the only option.

Like the police debate over race and crime, the courts have come under scrutiny in concerns about the over-representation of black people in crime statistics. These concerns have been expressed especially in the areas of the sentencing practices of the courts. For instance, the use of actuarial justice has also its own disadvantages and advantages for incriminating more young black people in the process of assessment. The criminological debates on this issue have amounted to conflicting viewpoints vis-à-vis the influence of race and the sentencing decisions of the courts (Bowling, B. and Phillips, C., (2000). Racism, Criminology. London: Harlow).

The problem of actuarial justice has more disadvantages than advantages, for instance the use of humans to make decisions, which may use the probabilities methods for labelling those who are not 'high risk' for incarceration or exclusion. Also, the criteria used in assessment are often too simplistic and a major concern is caused by the fact that users may rush decisions due to budgetary concerns, and in a politicised atmosphere the assessment is more likely to be influenced either by public views or by political persuasion. In the longer run actuarial risk assessment might be productive of the exclusion of known risk offenders who could serve their punishment in community work. No wonder Bill Beaumont in Risk Assessment and Prediction Research argued that based on ethical grounds, criminal prediction was unfashionable in a political democracy and non-violent environment, and that the established social order also covers matters of legal administration, ecclesiastical religious courts and gender violence. This chapter explores the reasons for which violent acts have been perpetrated in society as an attempt to try to understand the social priorities that governed such human interactions. Therefore, the main purpose here is to trace the history of violence in Europe in the middle ages and in African traditional society, mainly Rwanda because it is there where recent resort to the use of traditional legal proceedings enables us to examine the diverse influences leading to the crisis in former colonies and to define the concepts of violence.

The difference appears to be that the violence in Europe featured Christianity fighting for heretical beliefs, but in Africa it arose out of traditional ritual celebrations, as in various parts of African society evidence shows that in one area ritual celebration might be a good thing while in other areas it is bad and results in violence. Genital mutilation is the circumcision of girls aged between 10 and 21 years and the ritual now involves the removal of not only the clitoris but also the entire labia. According to medical experts, the removal of the labia is a new influence from other African tribes who remove the entire labia, in the belief that these sexual organs make females immoral in their marriage and unfaithful. However, it does not only cause excessive bleeding, but also exposes females to more chronic infections, painful sexual intercourse and more complications during childbirth.

Human history is littered with violence, which has always been present in society, and can be traceable to Biblical Old Testament days where violence was described in two ways. Acts of violence were first recorded in the book of Genesis, where it states that, when the earth was corrupt in God's sight and 'filled with violence', this was the reason given for the punitive flood. Second, it is human made, as history consistently identifies violence with the ruthless exercise of power, by actions involving physical force or unlawful intimidation, resulting in loss, injury or constraints on the unprotected.

To Steven Pinker and Gopal Singh, the psychology of the existence of political violence is a fractal phenomenon, visible at the scale of millennia, centuries, decades and years(links.jstor.org/sici?sici=097002 93(197601)4%3A6%3C3%3APOPV%3E2.0.CO%3B2-5). It applies over several orders of magnitude, from genocide to war to rioting to homicide to the treatment of children and animals. According to anthropologists like Lawrence Keeley, Stephen LeBlanc, Phillip Walker and Bruce Knauft, these factors combine to yield population-wide rates of death in tribal warfare that dwarf those of modern times (Ibid). Political correctness from the other end of the ideological spectrum has also distorted many people's conception of violence in early civilizations, namely those featured in the Bible (Pinker Steven). However, John Singer saw this as follows: 'part of the answer lies in the complex picture presented by the holistic, integrative approach to understanding human nature and its relations to its civilizational milieu. The main features of the civilizational approach should not be taken as what anthropologists call "ascriptive characteristics," that is, attributes and categories that remain stable and require no revision' (http://www.idrc.ca/en/ev-87930-201-1-Do-TOPIC.html).

The major challenge posed by the increase of violence is how to prevent or control it, which suggests another possibility: that the critical variable in the indulgence of violence is an overarching sense that life is cheap. Mankind's inhumanity to mankind has long been a subject for moralization. On the other hand, the use of violence is often coupled with plunder, often with deceit or stealing. Hab. 2:8 extends the warning to those who hold positions of responsibility in society never to shade the blood by the use of violence to the earth and all who dwell on earth and the opening of the New Testament in Luke 3:14 warns soldiers who guard the cities and the countries against any enemies' intrusion to use divine wisdom and to rob no one by violence.

The use of violence, in other words, is psychological. It can be argued as the only option where all forms of protest or expressions of a more civilised approach have failed. While sociologically violence is argued as the only method within the reach of the unprivileged, it is the only avenue of protest open to those under the rule of a dictatorship opposed to democratic means of change by the use of public majority vote. Where religious groups are forced to confront heretical teachings or pagan influence by rejecting all compromise, their course of action may even include persecution rather than tolerating immoral influences.

European forms of violence in the past involved religious inquisition, physical torture and persecution to save the souls of unbelievers. As a matter of fact, the more contagious form of violence is that sanctioned by society or those in power to use violence in the form of punishment. This will be argued as violence born out of rationalising justice, duly sanctioned by society, impartial and controlled law enforcement, in restraints of unlawful violence such as mob justice, and in benevolent constraints of the mentally insane. This why the next section examines the concept of violence in its theoretical modes, trying to distinguish the grounds and aims of violence before condemning all violent actions for reasons of intellectual classification or cultural taste.

Control and prevention of criminal violence in the middle ages

The main areas of enquiry focus on the historical ways in which forms of violence were articulated in European and African societies. Mention will be made of specific examples, such as Rwanda, as illustrative models of how different societies settle their differences. From a historical perspective, the literature, electronic journals and various interviewees confirm why violence is so rampant in ritual celebrations in various African societies, which is gradually increasing rather than decreasing in many ways, either through modern technology or by people in different cultures falling back on old ways. This confirms that violence develops through a combination of many things, some of which are traditional and religious beliefs and cultural ritual celebrations. It is the purpose of this chapter to show how both in the Middle Ages and more recently societies have battled with violence. This chapter does not suggest the best legal way of tackling the problem, but simply reminds us of where society has come from when we struggle to fix the violence problem.

The elements of violence in African society keep reappearing in some areas and are evidenced in the traditional ritual celebration of sacred religious beliefs, which govern not only daily affairs but people's activities. These are beliefs from the ancestors, in some cases including human sacrifice, which is now on the rise. It is important to recognise that these practices are associated with the current understanding of why violence in these former colonies cannot easily be eradicated. Development factors have not always been represented and international interests are involved in maintaining violence. According Victor Turner, rituals are 'formal behaviour for occasions not given over to technical routine, having reference to beliefs in mystical (or non-empirical) beings or powers regarded as the first and final causes of all effects'(Turner, V., (1982). From Ritual to Theatre and Back: the Human Seriousness of Play. New York: PAJ Publications, p.79)

With a mixtures of all these beliefs and the power for hunger, developing countries especially in Africa are still endangered with backward beliefs in mysticism. Bad governance turns out to be the product of a mixture of beliefs and the greed for power, which creates a rule of dictatorship where the system is one that constructs violence, where leaders apply dirty tricks to convince the wider population that they were elected in a free and democratic process, not even respecting parliamentary decisions and doing what they want without consulting any one.

So it seems that that the use of violence in former colonies is considered as being embedded in society where colonial authorities used force, which is history repeating itself and is relevant to what goes on today in relation to the social organisation of former colonial societies. Colonial ideological manipulation and dominant policies keep on reappearing in foreign policies now and then. The current violence starts as a local minor political dispute based on differences in party political opinions and ends up in political crisis where perpetrators of violence batter their victims or use harsh rules, control of media and deny opposition parties the right of public assembly and social well-being; the two overlap but are not exactly the same type of violence.

To a large extent, this is the situation that weakens democratic rule or intimidates MPs into working as a secret organisation from which they discuss national matters behind closed doors. It is usually argued that these are the signs of political dictatorship killing multiparty democracy, where the head of state threatens to discipline MPs who makes decisions contrary to party expectations. Even in Western countries these tactics are often used, but the difference is that if MPs rebel against their own party it does not cause long-term damage to them as individuals.

In a developed democracy the ruling party may realise that a proposed piece of legislation may be unpopular with the electorate, since MPs do not act on their own behalf but on behalf of their constituencies. Under the democratic deficit system in developing countries all political decisions are determined by the head of state and personalised. Just to cite one example, in Uganda during a meeting to discuss the Land Act (Amendments) Bill, 2007, the head of state said that he would fight Buganda NRM MPs who opposed the Bill, when it comes to the 2011 elections (Yasiin Mugerwa, Daily Monitor News, December 21 2008) This is a state in which the political party leadership has strong control over MPs, where parliamentary MPs are delegated what to do and say by the president and to act as his or her rubber stamp. In my opinion this leads to despair and disillusionment and a lack of democracy in the multiparty system of governance; it is this type of dictatorship that over controls people's rights, doubles the source of imaginary fears, and leads to social ostracism, brainwashing, withholding information and dictatorial pronouncements coupled with the threats that shamefully prevail in the twenty-first century.

This raises the question of why developing countries have lost the ability to complete in the economic development system. The intention of developmental theory is that collective political executive power has to share responsibility with the democratic state in operation as the parliament, as the key principle of collective responsibility ensures that the head of state is consulted about all important political decisions in the cabinet. The leadership so often generally desired by the population is that politicians act closely and cooperatively together, even when they have conflicts over policy differences in democratic strategies.

It is necessary to consider how have the foreign policies of developed industrial countries caused developing countries to remain stagnant without economic development. The appropriateness of political and development policies is most importantly in terms of the denial of individual human rights; second, a belief in the death penalty without considering the sanctity of life and the feelings of victims should be questioned; third, its appropriateness across a range of social-cultural contexts; fourth, the damage inflicted on the children and family for life, in contrast to the societal culture model that creates a peaceful environment of how one should live with respect and without torture; the final components are the modernising of traditional rituals and religious sacrifices, a sort of reasoning by analogy that extends the wide respect for democratic values that has not been explicitly addressed in the past.

The use of violence will always breed insecurity, never arriving at truth, justice or equilibrium, but always endlessly reproducing counter violence. The failure to act against it is contrary to democracy and represents the gross negligence and failure of society to modernise or abolish it, a failure that will be seen by those to come as cavalier at best, betrayal at worst.

The positive approach that is desirable widely promotes the general idea of human rights protection, but society is now at last becoming aware that a system of control that uses isolation, emotional manipulation and violence to ensure compliance is unsatisfactory (Yasiin Mugerwa, Daily Monitor News, December 21 2008). However, there are various contributory factors, in the main related to the social structural development background, traditional cultural beliefs and other religious influences from the Western Christian and Islamic world, where problems are caused by external violence in a society that is developmentally impoverished.

A government policy of violent or capital punishment is misinterpreted by the less educated who think that intimidation through exerting power and threat is the best way of controlling and preventing the repetition of a forbidden act. For example, religious or traditional cultures treated adulterers as criminals, and under Sharia law they are stoned to death. Mostly these measures deal with issues of personal status, such as marriage and divorce, while Sharia guidance on criminal law has largely been tempered with legislation that is seen as more modern or secular; generally adulterers are not stoned to death in the contemporary Middle East. On the other hand, in countries like Iran, Saudi Arabia and Somalia where they implement Sharia fully, adulterers continue to be stoned to death (Jeremy Okungui, Africa needs a standby army to deal with her conflicts, 4 East African perspective, Thursday, 13th November/2008).

In the past in some African traditional cultures, when an unmarried woman was pregnant she was forced into exile or killed secretly to prevent shame and disgrace to the family. Cultures such as this took a lengthy period of time to ascertain the exact truth, contrary to what was previously believed in that culture. This was the way society reasoned at this period, which demands that now we reason further to remove all forms of violence in society.

For this reason, effective leadership should be based on an assessment of an individual's qualities rather promoting individuals on the grounds of political partisanship, which is often the cause of past and present failures of development. In the twentieth century we saw the results of both improved human development and failed human development. All forms of development demand qualified and experienced leaders who can contribute effectiveness and a suitable system for developing human capacity and allowing freedom of expression. That means more than constructing bricks and mortar, but creating a peaceful environment where people after a hard day's work can feel at peace in their home without having to worry about their security.

Violence originates within individuals and gradually builds out of frustrating conditions, either poor relationships in society or where the individual's ability to cope with a crisis is at stake. Political conflicts in society are on the increase as a result of an accumulation of poor leadership and unjust policies, which cause tension within the system that eventually leads groups or individuals to violence, often as a result of societal systems that are brutal and wholly unethical. In the process, the individuals involved find it hard to cope and are incapable of the tasks assigned to them, because they are not the right people with suitable qualities or experience and the ability to harness leadership and developmental strategies effectively.

What Gopal Singh describes as the psychology of violence is clearly represented in the prevalence of limited resources for social services in the realm of political influence in developing countries, especially in community care (links.jstor.org/sici?sici=0970-0293(197601)4%3A6%3C3%3APOPV%3E2.0.CO%3B2-5). The whole situation must be seen in a political context, where the inadequate standards of governance in developing companies particularly poses imminent danger to millions of people. Consequently the use of violence relies more on political influence and less on national planning, which is viewed as the reason violence is on increase because people are trying to fight back against repressive regimes.

The reality of the latest events and present performance confirms the political developments outlined in this book: young people who lose respect and a feeling of their own worth in society and see no purpose in living are prone to accumulate grievances and to use violence against a government playing a role dictated by the foreign influence of sales of arms, which keeps dictators complying with foreign economic interests or ideology. Equally, it must be acknowledged that many developing countries find themselves in a position where they cannot control violence and political conflict. Cause and effect cannot be treated in a blanket manner when it comes to foreign policies for service provision, as has too often been the case in poor countries.

Ironically, one of the landmark sources of evidence of the continuing causes of tension is how previously, many communities in developing countries lived in communal organisations in voluntarily communitarian structures, a process that was reversed or destroyed by the introduction of a superstructure. It seems that the pattern that fits the current consensus among communities groups in developing countries, users and carers alike, is that the standard of available mainstream political care is unacceptable and that it is left to over-burdened community organisations to fill the void.

It is further argued that people living under these conditions are uncertain of the future, very fearful and terrified. It is arguable that the efficiency of the superstructure process has lacked the forceful political will to provide minimal resources, which is the reason that increasingly more people are led into a cycle of political crisis and the use of violence where successive governments have used the politics of exclusion and suppressed opposition groups, which retards efforts to respond effectively to a climate of changing external influence and development. Furthermore, the essential nature of many developing countries' ability to plan is also restricted in terms of foreign policies, the availability of developmental funds and the open-ended nature of references to ethnocentrism ideology.

For this reason, developing countries' attempts to surmount barriers to trade and push their perspective onto the competitive wider market have always met with resistance. Therefore, this situation makes it a necessity to call on the international community to respond in variable ways to the question of how development policies for pluralism could help to enable developmental stability in developing countries and render them less likely to escalate violence. Also, I will argue that the hidden ideological influences in foreign policies explain the root cause of grievances within the wider scope of political conflicts. According to Joseph Stiglitz this has led poor countries to inequality, poverty and little or no growth in much of the region, because they have been based on a fundamentally flawed concept of what makes a market economy work (http://www.twnside.org.sg/title/twe288f.htm).

Stiglitz blamed in particular the Washington consensus policies of deregulation, privatisation and liberalisation of trade and capital flows that is promoted and pushed by the International Monetary Fund and its economists, while often ignoring the roles of the market and the government, even under US-style capitalism. Calling for a new agenda for reform, Stiglitz stressed that there was no single alternative, nor should there be any attempt to promote a single agenda. Each country, he said, must choose the alternative appropriate for its conditions and its people, though some general principles and broad elements of an alternative agenda could be outlined. These principles and elements, Stiglitz said, would include social mobilisation, ensuring equity and creating a good business environment that not only attracts foreign investors but also provides a hospitable environment for domestic investors (Ibid.)

In the situation in which poor citizens find their hands tied, economists argue that open policies and a free trade market are vital safeguards to ensure that development is fair play, which in practice could reduce dictatorship and the kind of leadership that keeps populations in poverty. A report from Food and Agriculture Organisation Assistant Director General Hafez Ghanem recently revealed serious food shortages; although world food prices have dropped since early 2008, lower prices have not ended the food crisis in many poor countries (Daily Monitor, Uganda, Wednesday 10th December 2008).

If lower prices and the credit crunch associated with the development crisis force farmers to plant less food, another round of dramatic food prices could be unleashed. Yet these are areas shouldn't face a shortage of food, since they have the capacity to produce enough food to ensure that no child suffers from nutrition; evidence nevertheless shows that malnutrition is high because of pockets of hunger and famine.

Hunger and diseases, as well as people trapped in poverty, result in the use of violence as the only means to challenge a dictatorship. It is important to look to governments to provide a just system within a framework in which people can be safely governed in a relationship of cohesion with no foreign dominance. Good governance must always be based on the central issues of good policies to assess exactly how it serves the people.

There is a need to ask how to create the momentum that creates human development and correspondence with human rights to address both national and international social development hindrances to good policies and action plans. It is impossible to run on weak legs that cannot support the upper part of the body. The child who has a big head represents the many and good policies and plans, lean shoulders represent the weak or non-performing institutions, while emaciated legs reflect developing countries' weak implementation process, which allows wonderful policies and plans to remain on paper, in workshops and conference rooms.

In fact, another definition of development is that it is a country of workshops and conferences. Strategically focused policies are bandied about such as 'strategic diversity thinking', sustainable development, capacity development and in some societies gender mainstreaming, but these policies and plans have little impact on the ground. Leaders talk in workshops and conferences, in retreats conducted purportedly for capacity building of various institutions, so much so that attending workshops has now become an occupation for many developing countries.

There is no particular formula, but good governance is a political philosophy focused on the aim of development justice rather than a checklist. It should ensure the economic development of human life through capacity building among its citizens, the promotion of good governance, the promotion of power, politics and partnership, and state service delivery where people are able to become creative.

Many of the early development policies and laws were used to enforce relationships in development structures that were created by those who actually used them, the coloniser, where citizens only played the role of subject and where public participation was a fraud. On the other hand, a good development structure is one that is guided by the universal principles of accountability, negotiation, agreement and respect for all parties involved, none of which existed or was considered important during colonialism. The colonisers had weapons that outsmarted all the local arms. This was the rule of death: you complied, or you died.

It is argued that these were examples at an early stage of the introduction of the use of violence as a norm and that such was the way of military rule in the colonies, where there was no room for any other sentiment or feeling. It was at its apogee and its only outlet was a rampage of the most despicable, abominable and atrocious acts, inflicting only suffering on millions of colonised people. Colonisers informed the local leadership and the local population that their countries, culture, language and identity were no longer acceptable and criticised everything had existed of value to the people as either primitive or satanic.

It is perceived as relevant to the current situation that in that period people in colonies despised their own culture, language and beliefs as being no longer of any value. In a way, despising your own identity was like despising yourself. There and then, local people were compelled by the use of law and force to learn new languages, adopt new cultures and eat exotic imported food made in foreign countries, while their local raw materials were shipped to foreign countries. What they grew and produced in their countries did not belong to them; it belonged first to the colonisers who established the violent system.

Take the Democratic Republic of Congo (DRC) as an example, where serious concerns have been raised about security in the Great Lakes Region. As soon as the Congo attained independence, international powers intervened in search of control of its vast mineral resources and strategic location in Cold War geopolitics. The resulting conflict, in which mercenary forces were active, bled Congo dry. Neighbouring countries, including Uganda and other East African countries, participated in this war mostly by supporting the nationalist forces. The nationalist forces lost out to the merchants of war. The aggressors from outside even fought a bloody war over the loot and control of Congo. This crisis created doubts about the moral responsibility of the international community to respond to the increasing level of violence in the region and to crimes against humanity where one war after another is occurring in a cycle of human suffering. Raymond Plant was right to argue that, 'Most people would agree that perhaps the most basic demand is for internal and external defence: externally to prevent or deter external aggression, internally to prevent individuals transgressing rights such as the rights to life, to privacy, property and security' (Plant, R., 1988:24).

Changes in perspective and in the ideological and historical source of violence are relevant as political constraints in developing countries where political conflict is more likely to generate the use of militaristic rule. Political disintegration is caused by the policies of either big companies or foreign countries, which appear to reinforce and replicate the use of so-called developmental donations or grants given to dictators. That this perpetrates political conflicts is readily illustrated by looking at foreign interest in buying arms and other political interests observed in recent years in various developing countries such as Sierra Leone, Liberia, Sudan or DR Congo.

What has been happening globally has divided militants into various camps. The continuing use of violence in such forms has led to recruitment to militant factions reached the point of a potential tragedy. 'Radical militant' liberation terrorists believe in radical or revolutionary change as a reaction to wider political injustice. For instance, during Israel's bombing of Gaza, Iran's supreme leader Ayatollah Ali Khamenei decreed that anyone who died in the defence of Gaza would be deemed a martyr (http://uk.news.yahoo.com/18/2008123/twliranianians-raid-british-diplomatic-com3cd7efd-/htm). It is always illuminating to see cultural differences in the way people from the West, Middle East and Africa react. In the West, extremist parties such as those of a Fascist or Nazi ideology believe in radical or revolutionary change; in Islamic countries radicalism may be the only option; but in African countries under dictatorship guerrilla war is viewed as an appropriate reaction. Indeed, the differences in perspective explain how individuals or groups are forced into radicalism: people who under normal, stable leadership would not have taken up arms to fight are forced into radicalism in abnormal conditions where they regard doing so as the only option to liberate themselves from dehumanising conditions.

However, it may also be suggested that there is just as great a gulf between operations of development and control within development market systems that do not allow countries to participate equally in development, from the social control of the late nineteenth century to the renewal of development trade market control concerning industrialised countries. The system has evolved from the slave trade to colonialism and specific social forms of injustice embodied in developing countries. Social control operating in particular illustrations of a dysfunctional development structure still causes problems.

The methods of development control that are being applied are irrelevant and hopelessly inadequate. The best way to avoid conflict and the use of violence, whether you are dealing with staff, customers, investors or others, is first to understand how people work and how new ideas catch on in order to appreciate what makes for successful leadership strategies.

The study of different types of welfare regimes leads us to understand that, while advanced industrialised democracies are often faced with the same social issues, they have developed different approaches to dealing with them. Critically, one of the reasons that developing societies will always range behind in development it the recognisable extent to which social policies in developing countries are increasingly subject to global influences and also that it is hard to break through historical constraints on development. Even though there may be an absence of civil wars, the existence of a cartel arrangement between economic interests to limit competition by controlling the market, especially exclusionary trade, is a seriously decisive factor determining a lack of development. This not only paralyses the developing country's development, but also disarms governments and people of their progressive values.

In these circumstances, a child-like appeal for a pluralistic open market system that works for and responds to people's needs in society is understandable and forgivable. In political terms this is democracy voiced from various sources, which generally disagree with the continued use of violence to dominate countries. These voices also argue that it would be helpful to take the current crisis seriously as they formulate foreign policies, to reduce the level of violence and grievances.

Some religious and cultural laws demand modification, not necessarily abolition but conducting the law according to guidelines that protect human life and reinforce the fact that it is an immoral act to take away human life or to falsify an accusation leading to punishment.

I want to finish this chapter with the example of the DR Congo. There are 17,000 United Nations troops in the DRC; the rebel leader Laurent Nkunda has an estimated 5,000 troops, most of them child soldiers. A recently released report has accused the Kinshasa government of excessive repression of people perceived to be political opponents. The report further accuses Congolese President Laurent Kabila of ordering the killing of 500 people considered to be political opponents. Targeted victims of this brutality, according to the report, are people hailing from the Western part of the country. 'where the government lacks popularity' (http://uk.news.yahoo.com/18/2008123/twliranianians-raid-british-diplomatic-com3cd7efd-/htm.).

The DR Congo has been a global centre of attention following the eruption of fresh fighting between government forces and the National Congress for the Defence of the People (DNDP), led by Gen Nkunda. The report claims that at least 1000 people were detained and badly tortured in the run-up to Kabila's second anniversary as elected leader, and accuses international donors of keeping silent on the human rights atrocities taking place there. Of course, donors are not likely support those countries where there is no external interest. This is not just as a matter of principle, but because their money will be wasted and could be invested elsewhere.

Deaths such as these are not inevitable or random events beyond human control, they are the result of political choices taken (or not taken) by governments. These choices are influenced by cultural, development, environmental, social and political factors that governments and other actors can shape or mitigate. The behaviour of the UN Peacekeeping Force is setting a very bad precedent.

If the rich countries' gold and diamond traders can get out of Africa and if African blood diamonds can be boycotted on the world market, arms supplies will cease and African armed conflicts will reduce significantly. It is also high time that the continent had a standby army to deal with regional conflicts (http://www.stopvaw.org/Theories-of violence.html).

Chapter six

Crime prevention, community safety

The background of violence

This chapter examines the historical prevalence of violence and its roots in both European and African societies by looking at the causes of violence and its prevention from a legal point of view, as well as the religious and cultural context by using Rwanda as a traditional African model.

Crime prevention in Europe between 1200 -1550 AD

In England between 1200 and 1500AD King William I officially instituted the ecclesiastical courts. The law used to address crime in Europe was both Roman canonical law and customary law. The presiding judges were officially appointed by the Bishop, known as the Bishop's Commissary. In addition to that there was an appeal to the Court of Arches and there were several other courts like that of an archdeacon, of the Dean and on a parish level.

The ecclesiastical courts often involved an influx of lawyers trained in canon and Roman law. The judicial dimension was executed in itinerant courts, those of the bishop's commissary general and the archdeacon's visitation, as well as in diocesan consistory courts. The consistory met in the cathedral, where the session's officers and procedures were all established and recorded by scribes. In sharp contrast to common law and royal equity, ecclesiastical law existed for the ostensible purpose of moulding human behaviour to a transcendental standard. Like parliamentary statues, the canon law was a huge accretion of legislation prohibitions given renewed urgency in synod decrees and the summa for confessions (Baker, J.H., (1979). An Introduction to English Legal History, second edition, London: Butterworths, p.112).

The ecclesiastical court presumed the omnipresence of sin, which required judiciaries and public punishment in addition to the private sacramental purgation in confession. European legal history shows that in the period between 1200 and 1550, most cases recorded in ecclesiastical courts were matrimonial, while other cases were to do with alleged defamation and other charges of perjury, which meant breaches of simple contracts amounting to actions for debts.

In most jurisdictions, the remaining third of court business involved claims by parish priests for unpaid mortuary fees, allegations of violent assaults against priests, disputes over tithes, testamentary matters and occasional charges of heresy. The historical Western religious dimension of violence came during religious inquisitions and crusades, when there was physical torture and persecution in the name of saving the souls of non-believers. The notion of breaking canon law in the ecclesiastical court context implies that lawsuits were a potential breach of the social order. Other recorded charges were wilful murder, attacks on the property of the church, heterosexual promiscuity, non-cohabiting married couples, fornication, adultery and those who failed to attend the required number of masses each year.

The ecclesiastical courts were allowed to use two torts: laying violent hands on a clerk of Holy Orders, which was also a breach of king's peace, and defamation, which was not actionable at common law until the sixteenth century (Baker, J.H., (1979). An Introduction to English Legal History, second edition, London: Butterworths, p.112). The church developed these moral canonical law structures to provide restraints on members of society and to impose both confession (moral control) and paying tithes. However, the prominence of the ecclesiastical courts and its charges increased especially as a result of great numbers of allegations of forged wills. All this seems to suggest that it was a religious duty for individuals to act as their religious teaching expected them to act and to be answerable to religious institutions. Religious belief imposed moral restraints and individual responsibility for problems and individual actions in society.

Nevertheless, the main aim of the courts was not to punish but rather to act as a form of apparatus to correct sinful behaviour in society. The idea of the ecclesiastical court trial functioned as a remedy. Despite the fact that the trials increased wealth for the church, which was occasionally distributed to the poor, in theory and in the minds of laity the reason for having a court was more than the collection of wealth for the church. It was a reflection of God's commandments and how individuals ought to conduct themselves in all spheres of their life in society.

Specific orders were given for future avoidance of the same sin, and the church was always conscious of and concerned with personal salvation and showing ways and means of behaviour. During legal proceedings the emphasis of both the prosecutor and the defendant was on interpreting and arguing about matters of sacramental offices (Baker, J.H., (ed.) (1978). Legal Records and the Historian, Papers presented to the Cambridge Legal History Conference, 7-10 July 1975, and in Lincoln's Inn Old on July 1974, London: Royal Historical Society, p.91).

In the ecclesiastical courts sentencing or punishment was in most cases usually fines, public shaming or religious orders for discipline (i.e. to recite the Ten Commandments three times a day and repeat the Lord's Prayer four times) as away of imparting the Christian message to individuals. If the defendant was proven guilty of disobeying the punishment the court was forced to ex-communicate them, but this was only rarely used as a result of repeatedly criminal behaviours or a refusal to pay tithes. The whole emphasis of the trial was a form of religious moral restitution, as it was very much enshrined in canonical law to encourage an act of reconciliation to the person they have wronged.

As every legal system includes discipline, there are bound to be legal wrangles and bad feelings towards the judicial system. In this case the public reaction was mainly concerned with the financial ability to pay the exorbitant fines, to the extent that poorer people saw the court's role as church tax collectors and as exploitation. For example, the poor farmers of Kent revolted against the authorities and also caused bad feelings towards the church. In the opinion of the poor, rather than maintaining spiritual discipline and reconciliation, the emphasis of the church was diverted on wealth acquisition, which was regarded by the poorer as victimising them and creating unnecessary fines.

While the common law courts spent most of their judicial sessions actively and directly examining defendants regarding breaches of customary laws, in the feudal system there were several levels of courts, from the lords of the manor upwards. It is important to point out that at this period there were no legal rights to justice and even those who appeared on charges could not receive equal treatment. Secondly, failure to appear before the lord of the manor's courts a resulted in an arrest, imprisonment and confiscation of property. The jury trial was only introduced from the continent after the Norman conquests.

However, legal historians consider the true origin of the jury to be founded in the Frankish Inquest (inquisition), which was introduced by King William I. The adoption of a jury was to improve and bring justice to court trials and after its introduction it determined the whole future of English law. The jury system instituted an important principle of litigation before the court hearing. The jury inquest was a mode of obtaining, through royal authority, information or evidence that was required by the executive government. It was a directive to local officials to summon a number of persons from the district, who would examine the nature of the charges. It was a process of litigation for getting acquainted with the specific facts, and required the jury to attend on a royal officer and testify to the truth of the matter (Cfr. Kiralfy, A.K.R., (1958). Potter's outlines of English Legal History, London: Sweet & Maxwell Limited, p.121).

The jurors acted as witnesses, providing information about local issues, as proof of local customary issues was essential for trials. To qualify as a juror one had to be of good character that was proved by having no criminal record. Kiralfy observed that there were usually twelve men without any previous convictions or offences (legal hominess) (Ibid. p.125). From the nature of legal hominess a bad character could not be interrogated and the persons called as witnesses swore a very formal oath as to the truth or falsity of the facts of the claim.

The introduction of the role of jury

To start with the jury dealt with quite a number of cases, such as breaking of king's peace, disputes over land ownership and criminal cases such as violence, and dealt with business, properties and normal dealings between people. It also served the criminal law; Kiralfy observed that trial by jury dealt with violence, physical injury, theft and dangerous deception: 'It became a symbol of protection against arbitrary oppression; and even to the present system introduces the element of common sense into the administration of the criminal law' (Ibid.). The jury came at the right time, when it was badly needed, since courts were the only basis for deliberation on the charges brought forward for verdicts. In most the verdicts would be in favour of the accuser, which further suggests that often the voice of the powerful is taken as the truth.

Stenton noted that 'there were no records revealing more plainly the extent to which the Anglo-Norman judicial administration depends for its efficiency on the co-operation of English free men of repute, capable of giving good testimony' (Stenton, D.M., (1965). English Justice between the Norman Conquest and the Great Charter 1066-1215, London: George Allen & Unwin Ltd, p.52). The jury system normally fell into two categories: the civil jury was responsible for solving land disputes, while the grand criminal jury dealt with criminal charges. In murder charges, the jury had to show that accused's conduct caused the death. In a murder trial the (royal) court authorities summoned a number of people from the local area to assist the judge and to establish the nature of evidence, so that the court could be acquainted with the specific facts of the case.

Jurors were required to testify to the truth of the matter and this did not only apply in England, but also on the continent. In the king's courts the judges often examined the witnesses separately, after the manner of a canon of law inquisition, but this rationalisation came too late to make the formal witness trial a permanent rival to the trial jury. The court took no trouble to search for evidence, as it was the duty of the jurors to answer 'yes' or 'no' to the question put to them; they spoke from their own knowledge but not necessarily as eye-witnesses (Kiralfy, A.K.R., (1958). Potter's outlines of English Legal History, London: Sweet & Maxwell Limited, p.121).

It therefore become a challenge for the jury to establish the evidence of allegations before a court trial and this forced the jury to carry out their own inquest to establish the evidence about the incident before the trial. For example, Arnald pleaded not guilty to murder in 1421 and accepted trial by jury. The jury was summoned, but instead of giving a simple verdict, the jurors declared on oath the full account of what had happened between Arnald and John (the deceased) before the incident took place. After their detailed account, in the presence of the 'sheriffs and coroner of London', the jurors were asked if Arnald was guilty of murder and they said not. Arnald was spared and his case referred to the king's pardon (Calendar of Plea and Memoranda Rolls...of the City of London AD 1413-1437, ED. A, H. Thomas (Cambridge, 1943), p.114).

From this period gradually the jury began to take on more important judicial functions, moving from being witnesses to deliberating on evidence produced by the parties involved in the trial. According to Stenton, 'the demand for royal justice grew more rapidly than the king or his judges can ever have expected' (Ibid.).

In this period the role of the church in society was both spiritual and moral regarding the right way of conduct, rather than spiritual, while today the church's role in both spiritual and public conduct is very much more questionable. On the other hand, the use of punishment was rather public, shaming the guilty to make it clear to them that their action was not acceptable. Others were publically denounced and put to shame and ordered to wear a yellow ribbon or walk around the church for a given numbers of rounds.

The law and the moral code sometimes work together, but at other times the law gives no support to morals. The critique of the ecclesiastical court is that it is ludicrous to suppose that the form of punishing an offender highlights broader differences in terms of the emphasis of legality. While the ecclesiastical court's emphasis aimed at creating responsible members of society, an element may be regarded as repressive, authoritarian and greedy for wealth.

Punishment in modern society often drives a person to be a habitual offender. Once they are in prison, they learn, if they didn't know it already, that a massive underground economy exists and those from socially deprived circles will easily drift further into it as a means of furthering their 'career' to the extent that they survive by the use of violence. It would be ludicrous to suppose that a form of punishment is to shame them in a public place, which in modern society would be an abuse of human rights. It is even arguable that these methods of public humiliation and fining poor offenders with big fines or excommunication was one of the reasons that drove them to become outlaws of the Robin Hood type.

Nevertheless, by the end of the fifteenth century the two legal systems were not getting on well, especially the ecclesiastical courts under the authority of the pope and the King's Bench. At this period there were a number of complaints from those who had been sued in ecclesiastical courts rather than in the king's courts and this was due to where matters of charge overlapped the jurisdictional boundaries. In 1485 Huse declared that the king was answerable directly to God and was superior to the pope within the realm. The King's Bench gave a number of reasons why the ecclesiastical court was no longer needed: there were unnecessary delays before cases were heard and trials by the judge alone were unfair. It was further stated that the king's law had permitted the church court's jurisdiction only on trust, and that if that trust was abused that liberty was forfeited.

The rejection of Roman canon laws by the King's Bench had political implications. First, the pope's holding of both secular and ecclesiastical power was soon coming to an end. Second, it confirmed that secular power had exerted a great influence and control over the church in Europe. For instance, in Europe between 1286 and 1288 in Pistoia there were many nobles, among whom was a clan of powerful citizens and gentlemen, called the Cancellieri, which had eighteen knights and was so powerful that it defeated all others and they became so proud that they insulted everyone, committed many cruelties and had many people killed or wounded (Baker, J.H. 1979). In Germany the aristocratic influence was dominant; in France, the powers of the monarchy over church appointments and privileges had been significant; while in Britain a national church was emerging in which the pope's influence was severely restricted.

Despite the introduction of juries, but the legal system was still halfway to being a just system. Baker argued that the common law courts were the courts of the king and that therefore there was no justification for allowing appeals from the king to any one else (Ibid.). However, the defence given by Baker was that 'there was no possibility of human error in a judgement supported by divine intervention and therefore beyond questioning. Human judgement did not play a significant part in the resolution of disputes until the development of the jury as a fact-finding tribunal; but even the establishment of juries, and the consequent separation of findings of fact from rulings on law, did not result in the introduction of appeals (Baker, J.H. 1979).

African traditional prevention of crime and violence

A contrast between the early periods of European justice and the Rwanda Gacaca court used as a sample of the early judicial system before colonial rule shows how different societies respond to the question of crime. The justice system was described as a settlement for people and the focus was on diverting offenders away from the criminal justice culture, which was a key example of crime prevention and community safety at work. It embodies the idea of managerial performance targets and partnership/multiagency structures in the form of punishment centres. Felson observed a practical change in the nature of the situation, especially in industrial Western countries, where the construction of buildings denies or reduces opportunities for offenders to engage in deviance (Felson 1998).

This is the type of community involvement incorporated under the remit of restorative justice measures, which aim at breaking boundaries and criminal offences. However, do the sanctions of the structural approach work? Therefore, this section examines first the way in which the justice system defines the concept of effectiveness, second whether multi-agency working can be described as successful, and third the continuing tension between strategic diversion and criminalisation. Africa had customary laws with almost the same approach as the European ecclesiastical court structure and precedent; the only difference between the two was sentencing. I will illustrate with one system that has been recently restored after a long period without use as there were no other options. In Rwanda after the genocide the legal system had been completely destroyed, judges and lawyers had either been killed or were in exile and the country was faced with thousands of political conflict suspects. The president decided to consult community leaders to consider the right approach. It was agreed that the idea of traditional conflict resolution (Gacaca courts) should be restored, which was an effective form of traditional justice and law enforcement. Gacaca means lawn or lawn justice, named after the place where elders traditionally gathered to resolve family disputes. Traditionally, Rwanda recognised elders and entrusted them with the legitimacy of authority to mediate in family quarrels using the traditional method of dispute settlement known as Gacaca (Turnbull, C., 1984:102).

What is most important is that Gacaca proceedings are easily followed and originate in the home. I wish to argue that a legal system has no function in itself, but only when it plays a role in the society in which it exists. The legal authorities realised that the slowness of procedures and the long delay in bringing cases to trial represented a serious risk to hindering the reconciliation process, and therefore to national unity (Des Forges, Alison, 1999:3-7 http://www.developments. org.uk/data/Issue24/local-justice.htm/9/07). Des Forges argued that Rwandans must look for a way forward through Gacaca, seen as a compelling means of Rwandan expression.

It was necessary to classify differences in penalties, infringements and legal procedures for pleading guilty and, second, to establish measures to be adopted in order to speed up the trials. The approach of the Gacaca court was important in that it places emphasis on justice and the essential characteristics of the reconciliation process for all segments of society, requiring community participation to address collectively and simultaneously all the root causes of the conflict, thus contributing towards the healing of society.

The authority and effectiveness of this traditional system were reintroduced in the view of international law with regard to a fair trial, without prejudice to people who allegedly committed or conspired to have committed crimes that fall under the category of political conflict. The effectiveness of the system refers to the extent to which legal procedures were significantly delayed in their implementation, and the sheer scale of the killing meant that the process of bringing cases to court and determining appropriate penalties would be unacceptably protracted.

Gacaca courts were set up to establish the truth about what had happened (http://www.developments.org.uk/data 24/local-justice. htm/17/9/07) and to deal with the large numbers of perpetrators in a way that would allow for the involvement of the people and would satisfy the victims' desire for justice. The list of defendants could also be expanded to include representatives of other segments of Rwandan society that were particularly implicated in the atrocities. Gacaca court trials allowed suspects in the killings to be taken back to where it was alleged they committed their crimes and tried by a panel of judges chosen by local people (Newsline 006, 23–29 May 2005). In the Gacaca system the local population acts as witnesses and judges, and the whole community is encouraged to attend the trials (http://www.developments.org.uk/Issue24/local-justice.htm/17/06/07). The international tribunal had to follow the precedent, set by the Nuremberg trials, of hearing cases against the leaders, the central core of individuals who planned and organised the political conflict (Doyle, Mark, Ex-Rwandan PM revealed genocide planning, BBC News, 26 March 2004).

Given that the role of Gacaca courts is to satisfy the demands of justice as a necessary prerequisite for societal healing and reconciliation, the question to ask is what role the death penalty plays in this. At the early stage of the first trials in the immediate aftermath of genocide, there was a difficulty with the Rwandan theory of punishment as it involved the death penalty, which made it hard to identify the most appropriate form of punishment for use in this case. Indeed, some individuals and humanitarian organisations expressed their concern and objected to the death penalty as inappropriate for reconciliation.

Indeed, at this period a policy of non-violence was badly required in Rwanda, which by definition has the effect of perpetuating and strengthening the diversity of the political status quo. That is why the wonderful effect of non-violent punishment is encouraged for reconciliation: since encouraging revenge never changed the use of violence, this policy had to change, since it was unhelpful for uniting people in the country. Those who disagreed with the use of the death penalty argued about how to get rid of the illusion that the death penalty was above all a means of reducing crime, and that in this role, according to the reconciliation objective, was unthinkable.

It is argued that given the role of the rational choice of reconciliation and conflict resolution, the use of alternative, broader theoretical perspectives on behaviour change should emphasise interaction for reconciliation. Therefore, considering the Rwandan political situation and based on psychological theoretical perspectives, taking away another person's life is fundamentally an abuse of human rights (Human Rights, Art., 30). The rational argument for the idea of the death penalty is that it reduces the burden on government expenses and is an alternative to keeping offenders locked in prison. However, there is a powerful defence against such abuse of power. Michel Foucault in his prison research observed that power should not be used to dominate others, but to provide knowledge; power invests in people and there is no power without awareness (Foucault, M., 1980:17-23).

Regarding the death penalty, it is arguable that Foucault saw power as a positively constitutive force, for instance to restore individuals to society in a functional role for responsible citizenship. In this case, since knowledge constitutes reality, if all forms of knowledge are also forms of power, then the reality is that power can be both a negative and a positive constraining force depending on who possesses the knowledge or power. Thus it is argued that the use of the death penalty is a power that severely restricts the possibility of obtaining redress, towards the pursuit of individuals or the attribution of collective responsibility (Thomas, D. A., 1967: 455-503).

If the aim of the legal system is to transmit these values, the justice mechanism must also assist people to reconcile, rather than putting more weight on the use of violence or the death penalty. Torture still features prominently among human rights abuses in many countries, but the death penalty denies the right of human existence. In reference to human rights abuse the issue of the death penalty requires to be sorted out, and it was an impediment to the human rights cause. Rwanda rightly objected to the use of harsh treatment that contradicts the meaning of punishment. Human rights reports have highlighted people struck by fear caused by public executions, which have made many nervous about their treatment in the various countries that still apply the death penalty.

It is imperative for many countries to note example of Rwanda, a country that could have advocated for revenge but took a civilised response. Local respondentspreferred this alternative approach to uphold human values for the purposes of human punishment, one that focuses on a more sophisticated specification or restorative approach. From the restorative point of view, there were local arguments for a need to invest in a more satisfactory range of community-based forms of punishment, rehabilitation and reintegration into society in order to restore human relationships. Where such provision is compatible with the safety of the public, it seems to have a number of powerful advantages over the death penalty. One has only to point out some of the precautions to realise that capital punishment remains, even today, a spectacle that must be forbidden (Foucault, M., 1977:15).

It is also argued that in controlled punishment there is an element of denunciation and dealing with offenders, which is another way of making it clear to them that their actions were not acceptable, rather than simply taking away their life. Amnesty International emphatically rejects the death penalty, arguing that it is morally wrong to deny another person life, even if that person has taken away another life (Amnesty International, 3 January 1997 / Death penalty / unfair trial/9/11/07). So far, the only positive sign is that there has been a significant decline in the number of death sentences in Rwanda and a rise in acquittals since 1996. Nonetheless, over 650 individuals have received death sentences in Rwanda's specialised political conflict courts, 23 of whom were executed on 24 April 1998 (Ibid.)

The use of the death penalty created much public fear and led to expressions of concern that future trials would be unfair and similarly violate fundamental human rights. The trials admitted evidence that had an adverse effect on the fairness of the proceedings. Hearsay should automatically have been excluded. However, this does not mean that every case saw significant or substantial breaches of the judicial code of practice. Nor does it mean that the task of the court was merely to consider whether there would be an adverse effect on the fairness of the proceedings. Rwandan president Paul Kagame criticised the International Criminal Court of Rwanda, saying that it was doing too little and spending too much to try political conflict leaders, although he was grateful for the international support: 'The ICTR has for example spent a billion US dollars only to try about 32 cases; it sounds ridiculous to me' (New Vision, Ugandan newspaper, 9 November 2006).

The meaning of a Gacaca court and how it is regulated

A Gacaca court is run by elected officials based on traditional models. It is argued today that traditional Gacaca courts weren't so punitive, but were a way of restoring harmony (Cfr. http://www. developments.org.uk/Issue24/local-justice.htm). The main objective was to promote reconciliation and forgiveness (Amnesty International, 3 January 1997 / Death penalty / unfair trial.). The new Gacaca courts operate under Organic Law 40/2000(Cfr. Weblog.leidenuiv.nl/users/havemarch/archieves/2006/03/25/agacaca court-session.html).

In organic law, Gacaca court victims verbally vent their anger and the perpetrators stand accountable. Kayitana argues that it is a powerful means for resolving disputes in society, and adds that the issues considered were also social issues. This is because the reconciliation of the two parties was an important goal for the whole community. In itself, of course, the aim constrained the conduct of the court, as the decision reached had to be one that would not irrevocably alienate any member of the community. There was therefore a continual emphasis on reconciliation and compromise. The present Gacaca, unlike the previous one, demands information gathering, the contribution of interests and the participation of local communities in establishing the facts and determining the verdict and the sentence. The kind of justice carried out in the context of the Gacaca courts allows individual suspects to be identified by the accused. It allows the accused to offer a defence of his or her activities, such as being forced to kill under threat of death.

The aim of conducting trials in local areas is to provide the opportunity for a witness to come forward, since there were several witnesses and survivors who could clearly identify the perpetrators and give coherent and accurate descriptions and quantifiable evidence based on the individuals' actions and incidents. According to International Alert, the judge must be a respectable person of at least 21 years of age and elected by people of voting age (http://www.paraclete.us/rwanda/gacaca.php/11/9/07). He or she will be required to observe the judicial broad measures to establish the legal proceedings and guidelines for local trials (Cfr.http://www.ambarwaqnda.org.uk.genocide/insex.htm/11/9/07).The reason for implementing these local courts was to provide a quick and effective national judicial system. The newly appointed judges were charged with the task of regulating and supervising the courts to obtain fair trials without prejudice, and to determine how the tasks of investigation and prosecution should be decided. It was decided for the sake of a manageable caseload to divide the perpetrators into three levels of culpability. The central core was a tightly organised group of an estimated 100 to 300 people (Cfr. http://www.ambarwaqnda.org.uk.genocide/insex.htm/11/9/07). These people planned and organised the political conflict. This core, known as the 'zero network', included many close associates of the late President Habyarimana, as well as the political, military and development elite; beyond the capital, it included regional and local mayors, political party heads and militia leaders.

The present Gacaca identifies the suspects to the gathering and the indictment is read out. Then the Gacaca court listens to the evidence, passes judgment and sentences the guilty to serve the community (Ibid.). In the Gacaca court hearing, once the defendant is proven to have participated in political conflict, the legal burden shifts to the defendant to justify or excuse him- or herself (Cfr. [1935]. AC 462; SHC 42; Woolmington v Director of Public Prosecutions, p. 28). The legal requirements under which the Rwanda Gacaca court is conducted seem to be illustrated by the difference between the civil case and Gacaca trials, which like any criminal case, must be proved beyond reasonable doubt). Not all the members who sit on the panel speak, but the majority acts as a jury in a way that is similar to British legal proceedings. It is recommended that all hearings be 'open' and held in public to remove any suspicion about the fairness of the decisions made. Monitoring and supervision of the operation of Gacaca courts all over the country is carried out by the coordination department, ensuring that the system operates in a just way. What is positive about Gacaca hearings is that they are quite easy to follow, and the court process and hearings are very relaxed.

The fact finding is in fact a matter of common sense if a defendant who is faced with evidence fails to come forward and provide an answer. It is sometimes equally a matter of common sense that even where the prosecution has a prima facie case, an inference cannot be drawn from silence in every instance. Every case depends on the nature of the issue and the weight of evidence presented by the prosecution. In general, the atmosphere of this particular legal culture is structurally functional, focused on traditional interpretation and application. Under the Gacaca system, judges are selected from all parts of the country and sits in panels of 19 (http://www.developments.org.uk/Issue24/local-justice.htm/7/9/07). During my last visit to Rwanda in May 2004, I had the chance to interview members of the judiciary from the Gacaca reconciliation centre and from the faculty of law at Butare National University, who supervised the Gacaca court trials at Butare as part of the university training law centre. Elections for the Gacaca jurors took place in October 2001 and the process began in June 2002.

The Gacaca courts comprised men and women of integrity known as Inyangamugayo – individuals elected from the Hutu and Tutsi communities. By May 2004 there were 11,000 Gacaca courts spread over 106 districts in Rwanda. In addition, 254,000 judges were elected based on their integrity, conduct and non-involvement in the political conflict (http://www.developments.org.uk/Issue24/local-justice. htm/7/9/07).There was also a group of 209 Hutu and Tutsi women leaders responsible for informing the public when the Gacaca hearing was due to take place in local areas (http://www.internationalalert. org/pdfs/Rwanda%20%20Gacaca%20meeting.PDF/28/5/06).In 2003, International Alert and ProFemmes (Twesehamwe) formed umbrella groups for women's organisations, with over 4,000 members in Rwanda;(International Alert in Rwanda: Justice and reconciliation, Gacaca process, 28 May 2006) for ethical reasons I cannot name them. According to research sources, the Gacaca trials initially caused panic and speculation, and stress can prove too much to handle for some people. For instance, in Butare province there were speculations that the Gacaca court was an organised form of political conflict targeting the Hutus as a form of Tutsi revenge during the mourning period. The Gacaca courts were therefore initially met with fear and the disappearance of Hutus into exile (Newsline, 2006. This magazine mainly focuses on Gacaca trials, 23–29 May 2005, p. 13). This situation led to criticism by the UNCHR that the refugees were harassed and forced to come back against their will (Cfr. African Rights Appeal to the World Council of Churches contains a copy of the Bishop's Report 1999, p.9).

In this case, it was purely speculation and the role of women became very important, to reverse or discount the speculation and to encourage other women to come forward as witnesses, and not to live in fear or listen to any misleading information. This support provides witnesses with the courage to tell the truth about what they saw and heard during the 1994 political conflict (Newsline 2006, 23–29 May 2005,

p. 13.). A massive awareness-raising campaign was initiated in an effort to make sure that women from both ethnic groups play a major role in the Gacaca reconciliation trials. The main reason the campaign began was specifically to raise awareness about the origins of the conflict. The awareness programme also offers information about how to cope with the trauma of rape and widowhood. Among other things, women were trained as Gacaca judges, others to write articles in magazines, and others to produce radio and television programmes on subjects such as their experiences of political conflict, the history of the conflict and restoring community life (International-alert.Org/our-work/regional/great-lakes/Gacaca-procees.php/28/5/06). The functionary hierarchy of the Gacaca Court is as follows:

The general assembly is made up of local people over 18 years of age, who compiled a list of litigations for those who died during the political conflict, to record those who alleged that they had been tortured or raped, and to trace evidence from those who claim to have witnessed those who are suspected to have participated in the acts of political conflict. It is a process to record evidence that incriminates or exonerates suspects for having taken part in the political conflict.

The Gacaca court council operates as a coordinating committee composed of the chairman and two secretaries of the Gacaca court. (Cfr. http://www.ambarwanda.org.uk/genocide/index.htm). Gacaca courts at the village level only have the power to try cases of suspects who conspired to commit crimes that fell under category three of political conflict. Gacaca courts at parish level have the power to try cases of suspects who are accused to have conspired to commit category two political conflict crimes, while Gacaca courts at the district level hear the appeals of cases from the lower Gacaca courts.

The Gacaca court proceedings are generally informal compared with those in civil courts, so that the average person is more able to follow the whole proceedings of the trial. The language used in hearings is Kinyarwanda and sometimes French, and the whole arrangement is subjected to Article 6 of the International Tribunal on Human Rights, which guarantees the right to a fair trial. Another advantage to note here is that the Gacaca judiciary is made up of people who have expertise in the relevant geographical area, and are able to build up a depth of knowledge about that location that judges in civil courts could not achieve in such a short time.

Gacaca sentencing is mainly confined to those above 21 years old. There are various non-custodial sentences in the case of young offenders. When passing a custodial sentence, the Gacaca court is under an obligation to state the grounds on which it bases its decision, and how it reached that decision. The courts are allowed to acquit defendants and to pass sentences up to life imprisonment. The system allows courts to impose lower sentences for those who confess to their crimes, and jail terms can be halved if those convicted agree to do community service. Gacaca court proceedings are a form of participatory justice, where members of the public are offered the chance to speak out against those suspected, to give evidence, to judge and to punish those found guilty. It is important also to note that the process protects suspects from intimidation before and after adjudication hearings. In addition, it allows suspects to speak and be listened to during hearings, and for them to hear all the evidence against them. The procedure of the trial is introduced to suspects, and they get the chance to explain their actions and to question those laying charges and the relevant witnesses. Early findings suggest that those found guilty were judged fairly and consistently on the evidence before the adjudicating officer and after proper process (Cfr. http://www.marksbrain.com/blog/witnessing-gacaca/18/7/06).

Public response to Gacaca court trials

I decided to revisit Rwanda in July 2004 to observe whether there was any progress on the issue of justice, since respondents in the first interviews had vividly expressed this concern. I wanted to assess whether the Gacaca legal proceedings represented all ethnic groups and how it helped suspects to attain justice. Certain factors must be cited in explaining the considered rights of the accused to defend themselves and to see if there is any prejudice in the proceedings.

To assess the litigation process where the alleged offences took place many years ago, it may be possible to recollect evidence that was refuted in the charges and for the Gacaca court to handle such a situation. It was important to find out how the defence for the accused is conducted, and to assess the performance of the judges and the jury. This was a challenge to both judicial and reconciliatory groups. I was informed that the government had to play a high level of diplomacy in order to convince refugees to repatriate themselves back to their homes. In many rural areas the Gacaca legal proceedings made more sense than the Western legal system, and were easily accepted and used by local communities after their inception. According to both local respondents and a report from International Alert, the Gacaca system is seen in the eyes of those longing for justice to be a good approach (http://www.paraclete.us/rwanda/gacaca.php/18/7/06). However, with respect to the decisions and court deliberations, it is arguable whether Gacaca is an impartial system. According to International Alert, 'In 2004 the Gacaca laws were revised to respond to some of the criticisms of the pilot phase, which had been using the outcomes of the awareness raising meetings, we lobbied for changes to the laws through attending with parliamentarians and with the National Service for the Gacaca Courts' (Work by International Alert in Rwanda: Justice and Reconciliation- the Gacaca process 28/05/2006, p.1). One respondent who said that he was a moderate Hutu argued, 'Justice and accountability has to be established in regards to the individual suspects accused as perpetrators' (Special Report, Rwanda: Accountability for War Crimes and Genocide, A Report on a United States Institute of Peace Conference (2001), p. 1).

Evidence of this is perhaps the early acceptance of Gacaca courts by the public. Perhaps the reason for this acceptance was that they was not seen as intimidating, with no complex civil court proceedings, which makes sense in a non-literate culture where the hearing depends heavily on witnesses rather than on written evidence. Individuals who had made public accusations against perpetrators following the trials of political conflict were encouraged to come forward to give evidence in local courts in order to deter any further allegations. Accordingly, the quality of the proceedings has continued to improve, as has the administration of justice, although there are variations from one place to another. Based on observations and respondents' views, the Gacaca system is widely accepted by the public, but as long as the trials are subject to the supervision of the high court. However, there are still problems with the Gacaca courts. Mark Wagner's report suggests that there were incidents where witnesses were intimidated and murdered. His report also asserts that suspects were without legal defence, so that there is potential for violations of the rights of the suspects accused (Cfr. http://www.marksbrain.com/blog/witnessing-gacaca/18/7/06).

In addition, suspects in prison facing serious charges should be given time to prepare their case and receive advice where necessary. The measures were intended to help both sides, who may have difficulty understanding the procedures (Cfr. http://www.marksbrain.com/blog/witnessing-gacaca/18/7/06).Having looked at the court hearings, judgments and sentencing, this brings us to another crucial element of the public response to the Gacaca court trials: the process was too slow, with only 10 per cent of the courts around the country being held in each village. Wagner and Jerri also observed that there were other irregularities, such as judges failing to complete paperwork on time (Cfr. http://www.Marksbrain.com/blog/witnessing-gacaca/18/7/06). The critiques of Gacaca courts have pointed to the fact that without professional prosecutors, evidence and important testimonies were likely to be missed or mishandled. In their view, the process would create greater potential for the guilty to be found innocent or given an unduly light sentence (Cfr. http://www.Marksbrain.com/blog/witnessing-gacaca/18/7/06).

In my view, if the system were to be reconstructed in the way that was proposed by Wagner and Jerri, a higher priority would inevitably be on balance, creating a viable solution to a complex problem, but that takes time and needs to develop and be consolidated. Nevertheless, from my own observations, despite the bad start great changes have been made. Even if some areas were disorganised at times, there were signs of improvement, especially after the national Gacaca law was amended to address irregularities, such as judges' failure to properly complete paperwork. Finally, it is argued that under these arrangements, the Gacaca courts become an invitation for the public to respond by using them. This chapter has examined both the European middle ages and Christian and African legal systems, in particular traditional Rwandan ways of dealing with violent crimes. It has explained the use of Roman canon law and Organic Law 40/2000 practiced by Gacaca courts, and their relevance and legitimisation.

The chapter has looked at different kinds of approach to the question of establishing justice and reconciliation. It has described what people in communities are saying about the way forward in the search for a meaningful political solution to the conflict. The idea of Gacaca law as interpreted reality underlines the necessity of understanding the means by which other cultures resolve crimes related to violence (Cfr. Llewellyn, K. and Hoebel, E., (1941). The Cheyenne Way, Oklahoma City: University of Oklahoma Press, p. 127). In contrast to European law, Gacaca court used a similar approach of narration in several locations, because the fundamental need was for hearing tales or stories by witnesses in Gacaca courts as a means of assurance of justice, and avoiding any cover-ups or using short cuts to justice. Its main objectives were to amplify the matter outlined in the writ and to reveal a full cause of action. The Gacaca court addresses the issue of justice as a means of strengthening the judicial procedure, restoring community values and eradicating social-political problems.

It is equally essential in the process of securing genuine justice to consider people's culture and their customs (Interviewing University Lecturers at the School of Law May 2004.). It is argued that it is important to understand the relevance of the dispute resolution mechanisms of Rwandan culture because the danger of suppressing the need for familiar justice would only increase the fear and people concerned may recoil. In the final analysis, the establishment of the Gacaca courts did not only aim at punishing infringements, but also at re-establishing concord. The traditional law in the Gacaca courts provides for a range of penalties, (Cfr. http://www.ambarwanda.org.uk/genocide/index.htm/9/9/07) and the emphasis is on reconciliation rather than punishment. This is why the Gacaca legal process has adopted a method of 'Open Forum', similar to that of the South African Truth and Reconciliation Commission. The only difference in the two conceptions is that the Gacaca reconciliation argues that there are two important steps to take: first, to re-establish justice through the judicial system; second, reconciliation, which in Gacaca means naming the political conflict, mitigating the allegations and disciplining the perpetrators (Ibid.). The next chapter will make an attempt to access the question of violence sanctioned by the state to explore the meaning of punishment.

Chapter seven

Punishment and the death penalty

The rationale for sanctioned violence by society

In this chapter attention shifts to the use of violence, since this issue has kept both developed and developing countries in continual conflict. The debate on violence takes place over forms of punishment. On the one hand, there are philosophical and jurisprudential issues concerning the nature of the death penalty as a form of punishment principle. The argument is that the dangers of the misuse of punishments are a trend concerning the functional role of punishment systems in society, which is discounted by empirical and sociological studies that focus on the implication of the death penalty in practice. These approaches are more concerned with how the insinuation of capital punishment might be used in an arbitrary or discriminatory way, at the expense of members of other races or in case of minority communities, the poor, or other marginalised or politically disadvantaged groups in various societies.

In this chapter, I will examine arguments both for and against the death penalty, and discuss the claim that, when matters of principle and practice are brought together, they reveal the death penalty to be a wholly irrational system of punishment that purports to be rational. However, the most disturbing violence of our time is that reported by some greedy rich African people who ritually murder children for sacrifices to accord with their satanic beliefs, a practice that is on the rise in various parties of Africa. My views are quite clear that I hate any sort of violence, including the use of death penalty as a means of punishment. The death penalty in practice is very degrading to use in a civilised environment, for instance it is shame that countries like the USA still use this method as a punishment, because it is so dehumanising and an evil method, which should not be expected, even in wild societies where there are no legal systems. This is to suggest that the task for politicians is to keep a constant check on any loopholes and to analyse the causes of the conflict more than the process of reconciliation.

The question that follows is how perpetrators of child sacrifice should be treated. In my opinion, these people should first be examined medically to prove that their mental ability was not impaired by health conditions or the influence of drugs. If found guilty and they are medically fit and in sound mind, then their freedom must be denied and the punishment must be life imprisonment, in order to protect children and to inform the public that such people are a danger and not acceptable in society. But if an offender is found to have a mental deficiency and not be in sound mind, then he or she must be given a chance for rehabilitation in prison, where the prison officials and medical treatment will continually monitor any progress before final release.

One can think of the political crisis as deeply influenced by both the history of the colonial ideological culture of violence and the ethnocentric beliefs used in colonial policies. It is, rather, in the historical ideological policies most of the current conflicts are traceable. Therefore this stereotyping of politics contains the crisis in that the causes of grievances is that people's feelings and concerns and disregarded and they become entrenched in the conflict. Attention must be focused on the interpretation of the beliefs of racial superiority and the theories that were used to dominate other races by the use of law and dominant force to subject other races to dysfunctional behaviour. An overwhelming mass of literature is available dealing with various ways related to the use of force by prisoner officers, the police and the military forces, all of which fall under control of governments.

I will discuss why the developing countries have been caught up in political crises since 1945. The conflicts that have transpired have been mostly internal and not just between these countries and their neighbours. They range over wars regarding religion, liberation, rebellion and civil wars, to name a few. I will consider these conflicts and their make-up with regard to countries involved in the most serious conflicts along with the impact on dysfunctional economic infrastructures, and how these wars have been fought (Pearce, W., Barret, & Littlejhn, Stephen, W., 1997: 1-7).

There have been over 9.5 million refugees and hundreds and thousands of people have been slaughtered in Africa as a result of wars and conflicts (globalissues.org.). For example, many different groups in Angola continue to fight for resources, with industrial developed country governments supporting their actions. The need for raw materials from the land is often responsible for groups within countries battling for their stake in them (Ibid.). The rich resources alone are not the root cause of internal conflict. Political corruption, human rights violations and no laws being followed all have a hand in civil wars and conflicts (Pearce, W., Barret, & Littlejhn, Stephen, W., 1997: 1-7).

Those perpetrating the violence have also abused human rights by enlisting boys as young as ten years old to fight for the rebel groups. Despite any peace agreements, Human Rights Watch reported that human rights abuses were still taking place. Ethiopia and Eritrea are two countries that have had continuous battles over their border controls, especially when Eritrea wanted to become an independent country. Triggers are events that set off a conflict, pivotal factors that lay the foundation for the conflict, mobilising factors that have to do with which groups go into the conflict and aggravating factors. The above issues were considered as I discuss various countries within the third world and their civil wars and conflicts (Pearce, W., Barret, & Littlejhn, Stephen, W., 1997: 1-7.).

This chapter traces the signs of any persistence in conflict and the reasons, in order to show the cause of crises through an attempt to understand a number of issues linked to previous wider concepts, developed mainly in an earlier period of colonialism. Foreign development and international legal decisions are interlinked with wider issues, either because dominated nations are not performing as expected nor as their international legal obligations, but because the performance of the dominated nations is defective based on the dominant development interest.

As just a snapshot of the whole episode, in the 1400s European traders and settlers first arrived in West Africa. They established the African slave trade, destroying the region's population and economy.

Today, the descendants of West Africans and the slave trade are a significant population in Latin America, South America, North America and the Caribbean. During the nineteenth century, a series of violent struggles in the region resulted in the French and British defeat of local kingdoms. By 1900, most of the West African empires had been supplanted by European colonial rule. Senegal, Guinea, Mali, Burkina Faso, Benin, Niger and the Ivory Coast were united into French West Africa, while Britain colonized Gambia, Ghana, Nigeria and Sierra Leone. Portugal controlled Guinea-Bissau, and Germany ruled Togo until World War I. The former United States' colony of Liberia was the only West African territory to maintain its independence during the colonial era. After World War II, nationalism increased in West Africa. Ghana became the first sub-Saharan colony to become independent in 1957 (http: www.pbs.org/independent/ironladies/WestAfrica. html/312/08).

Violence has existed in society from the first day of human existence (Gen. 6:11). The introduction of technology has both good and bad aspects: it has advanced knowledge for rapid growth in communication and business transactions, but however good it might be it has contributed to an increase of violence in society.

The central focus of this book concentrates on the use of violence and the root of violence through ethnocentrism beliefs and theories to which developing countries have been subjected since slavery and colonial periods. This is the process of trying to re-examine theories of superiority, modern changes, the development of ideological capitalism and the belief in punishment. Wider issues have contributed to many young people in developing societies thinking that the use of violence occurs as a result of law enforcement, in wars and from state-sanctioned violence or punishment (the death penalty), and since then violence has become part of the tragic failure to find more humane solutions to human problems.

In considering these issues, it is helpful to bear in mind the mythology of violence being a result of a non-civilised culture or biological criminality originating from the culture of an underachieving black race. I will proceed to consider whether this is true, and compare and contrast the belief in superiority with what happened in the past and still happened today. This in turn will lead to consideration of these claims traced in the political ideological theories of social administration, both historically and recently in order to assess whether the use of law and development structures, attitudes, theories and beliefs has restricted other races from performing as expected.

Analysis of the implications of the wider dominance of industrial development policies in an international setting poses fundamental political difficulties such as developing the ability to play an effective role, when the only role they can play is to service massive debts. The worsening economic situation for the last 50 years has contributed to civil strife and has had a deleterious effect on the population, in which violence is rampant in search for alternative leadership to save them from poverty. There is now also the beginning of a hard landing in emerging markets as the recession in advanced economies, falling commodity prices and capital flight take their toll on growth.

For instance, slack labour markets with increasing rising unemployment rates will cap wage and labour costs. Policymakers will have to worry about a strange beast called 'stag-deflation' (a combination of economic stagnation/recession and deflation); about liquidity traps (when official interest rates become so close to zero that traditional monetary policy loses its effectiveness); and about debt deflation (the rise in the real value of nominal debts, increasing the risk of bankruptcy for distressed households, firms, financial institutions, and governments). With traditional monetary policy becoming less effective, non-traditional policy tools aimed at generating greater liquidity and credit (via quantitative easing and direct central bank purchases of private illiquid assets) will become necessary.

As banks curtail lending to each other, to other financial institutions and to the corporate sector, central banks are becoming the only lenders around. Given the severity of this economic and financial crisis, financial markets will not mend for a while. In a search for an all-embracing concept, Stohr indicates that 'developments could be considered again as an integral organisation of communities at the small and intermediate scales' (Stohr, 1981:11).

Certainly, confidence in the financial system has been battered. The integrity of many banks has been called into question. Many people have lost their life savings. Every year across the developing world, billions of dollars that are badly needed for health care, schools, clean water and infrastructure are stolen or lost through bribes and other misdeeds. This situation makes it harder to provide basic services and achieve the Millennium development goals even in the West, thus denying people their fundamental human rights (Ibid.).

This state of affairs probably explains the series of political conflicts that are the source of famine and civil war. Cultural shifts are continually challenging any possibility of development in developing countries, as well as leading to a failure to find out what is happening on the front lines of political change. Various voices today in developing countries argue for a need for an appropriate response given the high priority allocated to peace and diversity policies as key aspects for development, based on the rapid increase of violence related to historical coercion and subjugation of other races. The imposition of the rule of ideas in this matter is not at all concerned with the solution for an end to development dominance and control in developing countries. Paradoxically, the apparent foreign policies of Western countries are themselves political, because they play a role that is functional to a continuation of ideological policies of dominance that are problematic to achieving the peaceful stability that is effective for development.

The response of powerful industrial countries

The analysis here focuses on the wider implications of radical violent developments and the rise of militant beliefs and theories that are no longer tied to some notion of racial identity or roots, but that form part of a post-modern politics in which the development trading system is conservative and dominated by governments, banks and large companies looking to hedge against potential losses. This approach attempts to assess the external dominant influence and its correspondence with the historical colonial ideology and the current foreign policies of industrial nations. As we shall see later, the main connecting thread between militant groups is the question of wider political issues seen as injustice caused by racial belief in superiority on the part of industrial countries.

Developing countries can make a profound contribution to development and social service improvement, and play a positive role in building democratic societies where peace and stability are achievable. While writing this book I sensed the spirit of joint effort from countries recovering from wars and working at trying to combat poverty and I felt that, if there were no other factors, such actions are very helpful in bringing together people who share needs, hopes and dreams. These signs of a desire for self-reliance show themselves in the arena of their action.

This is argued as a core means of addressing violence in society, similar to Jimmy Carter's idea that seeks to 'prevent and resolve conflicts, enhance freedom and democracy, and improve health' (http://www. cartercenter.org/homepage.html). In order to prevent human rights violations, industrial countries, must support appropriate development policies that respond to the crisis in the world context to establish a development order where all countries exchange goods, services and trade without dominance, responding with realistic civilising conduct. The importance of this approach is seen as providing a less costly solution in terms of human life and avoiding recourse to alternative ways of finding an answer to the current world crisis, where our young soldiers are constantly losing their lives.

The significance of these struggles has highlighted the fact that to resolve the crisis requires more than a military solution. Sustained political initiatives are required to tackle not only the immediate grievances of the civilian population but also the long-term issue of political and development resettlement, which has long-standing historical roots. The historical accounts show a critical assessment of these issues and invariably demonstrate that industrial powerful countries' attempts to resolve historical and contemporary grievances will need to apply sufficient diversified comprehensive policies and will inevitably require the adoption of a new approach. Harriet Lerner argues for responsibility in this way: It is the ability to observe ourselves and others in interaction and to respond to a familiar situation in a new and different way (Lerner, H., 1990:17).

Thus, Western countries' development system will have to provide every nation with an opportunity to make their development contribution to a system that entails a fair distribution of the instruments of power in every country.

A constructive task would be a review of foreign policies and the use of a different approach that respects independence of other nations and promotes human values to arrive at a wider compromise solution.

In order to resolve the present crisis in developing countries, there is a requirement for a common position among all Western countries to provide a concerted response to this unprecedented political crisis, which can be a very useful and very promising civilized response.

In a period of historical challenge industrial leaders face the difficulty of successfully integrating into a society far more diverse than any we have known before; responding to that challenge requires world leaders to be both imaginative and sensible, and to ensure a balance between acknowledging the aspirations of developing nations and safeguarding the rights of vulnerable fellow human beings. All nations can face human development together and in time the crisis can be overcome if all countries take firm, decisive and effective measures in a responsible and timely way.

If the international community boosts coordination and cooperation and helps nations to trust each other, it will create mutual respect for all cultures as capable of contributing to the development of one world and a common economy, which I think is the right approach to stabilising development and promoting stability. Investors could ultimately be motivated by world stability to help deliver development to those whose chances have been denied for so long, so that should now be a key focus.

It is also argued that cooperation among other countries, especially in clarifying the role of government, companies and regulators to ensure financial stability, will be needed to properly handle the relationship between savings and consumption, or accumulation and consumption. With the emergence after World War II of the newly independent nations of the Third World, the problem of promoting development growth came to the fore. Development historians responded to this challenge by advocating industrialization, basing their arguments on the historical experience of the handful of countries that accounted for the bulk of their research -- the United Kingdom, United States, Germany, France, Russia and Japan (Richard A. Easterlin is the former president of both the Economic History Association and the Population Association of America. He is author of Growth Triumphant: The Twenty-First Century in Historical Perspective and Birth and Fortune: The Impact of Numbers on Personal Welfare).

Economists characteristically turned to theory, arguing the need for higher savings rates, as demonstrated by the Harrod-Domar re-model of short-term Keynesian theory. Some social scientists, impressed by the cultural disparities between East and West, questioned whether Third World development was even a realistic possibility. This highlights a need to keep savings and consumption at a normal, balanced and coordinated relationship in mutual agreement and negotiated by all countries. It is only through recognition in this way that countries can coordinate development stability. Countries must also coordinate the virtual economy with healthy development of the real economy, which will facilitate the growth of united development (Ibid.).

If all countries can work together, the causes of the development crisis, which has no precedents, will not continue to be reproduced in the political conflicts of the third world. It is this sort of remedy that must be encouraged in industrial countries, providing developmental funds as well as more effort to allow developing nations to supervise and regulate their developments without outside interference and keep them accountable.

A warning from developing countries is that all countries need to strengthen their oversight and crisis management mechanisms. The IMF may have to set up major credit lines to bolster emerging economies and help the world's poor countries affected by the conflict crisis. The response of the international community is often criticized for being too slow to recognize problems and for doing too little too late, especially when help it is most needed to avoid repeating the past.

While traditional fiscal policy (government spending and tax cuts) will be pursued aggressively, non-traditional fiscal policy (expenditure to bail out financial institutions, lenders and borrowers) will also become increasingly important. If the deficits are monetised by central banks, inflation will follow short-term deflationary pressures; if they are financed by debt, the long-term solvency of some governments may be at stake unless medium-term fiscal discipline is restored.

What is needed is a framework that provides stability in governance plus plays an important part in the reduction of military defence spending, the allocation of scarce resources and the creation of wealth to engage young people in creative activities rather than radical politics. Industrial dominant countries should study the sources of uprisings, civil war and ethnic conflict as a sign of continual negotiation and struggle over the boundaries of the dominant race and its otherness in contact, just as it continues to inform the shifting landscape of the dominance culture that has surrounded and generated ethnocentric theoretical perspectives that have been practised in the foreign policies of developing countries.

For better or for worse, developing countries become increasingly pushed into politically radicalised turmoil, so that to people in these countries the use of violence is argued as a long-term influence springing from the dominance of a colonial ideology embedded in the systems of politics, education and economics. Such a structure has persisted, is the source of the violent crisis today and keeps on causing racism, ethnic tension, victimisation and violence. The theory of superiority is a key point that needs further examination to identify how human relations have deteriorated and to show that there is something more that industrial nations can do to reverse these policies and modify external influences on internal leadership to end the use of violence.

Implications of the use of violence

This section highlights the sanctioned use of violence in the form of punishment and argues the function and the role of the punishment system in today's society. The aim of this is to explain the implications of the use of the death penalty, with consideration of how it can easily be prejudicial in the process of obtaining fair and impartial justice. In certain political circumstances punishment could be used as a tool of discrimination at the expense of minority members or opposition opponents, the poor and any other marginalised or politically disadvantaged groups in society.

This section will attempt to analyse issues involved in the process of implementing the death penalty and to advance this practice as the immoral and primitive treatment of another human being wherever it is still used as a form of punishment in the twenty-first century. It will try to use observed findings to illustrate whether the punishment serves the purpose of deterrence of a possible future offence by others in society. The use of the death penalty as a deterrent for crime has never worked anywhere and also presents its own major problems. It punishes the whole family rather than just the guilty person. Families suffer emotionally and financially; the public should also recognise that relations between the victim and the family of the suspected murderer may be stained forever. A brief explanation of a hypothetical consideration for the basis for taking a person's life is argued as a miscarriage of justice and criminal murder trials are also discussed. The discussion will highlight the influences and interferences of politics, the media, the public and the legal system in the process of trial.

Roger Hood throws light on issues surrounding the death penalty as it is still used as a punishment worldwide. He exposes the fact that increasing numbers of countries have abolished the death penalty, while others have reintroduced it. There has been both expansion and contraction in the range of offences subject to the death penalty and the extent to which states abide by the United Nations' Convention on Human Rights. There is also extensive written literature in the United States concerning legal, ethical and public attitudes towards the use of capital punishment. Existing Human Rights Acts and World Health Organisation statements offer guidelines, particularly in declaring principles about the way in which suspects are tried and treated by society.

The death penalty

This subheading examines more closely the effect and impact of the use of the death penalty as a form of punishment, the concept of partnership or multi-agency, and the use of evidence to define and find the guilty person. In particular, it focuses on whether these institutional structures and ways of finding someone guilty are non-prejudicial, without impartiality and pragmatic, or whether they are defined by ideological interests and centralisation; in particular, the section focuses on the influence of neo-liberalism in punishment making and administering.

The Death Penalty Information Center in the US estimates that 111 defendants will be sentenced to death this year. This cruel action signifies the relative steadiness of the figure of those subject to state-sanctioned killing since executions were reinstated in 1976; 37 people were put to death in 2008, compared with a record amount of 98 executions in 1999.

Currently, 36 states and the federal government have the death penalty. However, Nebraska's highest court found that hanging, the state's sole method of execution, was 'cruel and unusual punishment', leaving lawmakers at odds as to whether to replace it with lethal injection or prohibit executions altogether (CNN.COM/11/12/08).

The punishments for those convicted of murder have varied from one place to another, especially in the way the punishment is administered. For instance, in ancient days murderous criminals were either fed to hungry animals, shot in public or stoned to death, which is similar to what happens today under Sharia law. In general terms society has slowly developed from the punishment in the public arena to private punishment by either hanging or the use of injection or electronic means. In my opinion all this is done in the belief that the crude method used will deter others, but that where the death penalty is still practised it is a barbaric act. I condemn anyone who takes another person's life, be it an individual or a state.

The argument of those behind the death penalty is that it is a way to deter others from committing a similar offence. In my opinion the punishment must not equate with taking another life, but rather there should be an element of denouncing the offender, in order to make it clear to those proved guilty and society at large that the action is not acceptable. What in fact the death penalty confirms for those convicted is that violence is right in stronger hands. What is morally objectionable is that for the purposes of deterrence, one human being is treated as an object lesson rather than as a person. It is simply a devaluation of human life, which is utterly repugnant to human reason. Whenever we see one life treated like that we know that our own lives likewise have been reduced to that level.

However, I do not want create the impression that I am suggesting that the offender should be set free. Similarly, in the interests of safeguarding the public the right practice should put the emphasis on controlling crime by protecting the suspects from vengeance and the victims from the possibility of any further victimisation. In the earliest societies protection and vindication of victims, out of love towards them and indignation against wrong doing, were a societal responsibility and there was a duty to treat each human life the same as any other.

In poor countries where a suspect cannot afford legal expenses, in murder cases the state, as God's agency of vengeance (Rom. 13:1-

4), must assist suspects to help ensure impartiality and equity, providing them with legal representatives so that they can have a free and impartial trial without any outside influence. They need to be disciplined or punished without malice, and with an examination of the circumstances, motives and background of the offender. It is a religious or Christian duty to ensure the respect of human of life and the suspect must be protected from any harm or torture during the interrogation or mitigation period.

George L. Kelling, an Adjunct Fellow at the Manhattan Institute for Policy Research, has co-authored his latest book, Fixing Broken Windows, with Catherine M. Coles, a lawyer and urban anthropologist. Instead of reacting to crime, Fixing Broken Windows champions crime prevention. The impact of Kelling's and Coles' ideas will only multiply exponentially as Fixing Broken Windows gains national recognition. Kelling was a key member of the New York City Transit Police Team that worked to clean up the subway system. He has also consulted on crime prevention projects in numerous cities including Newark, Kansas City, Seattle, San Francisco, and Baltimore (Green, J. A., 1999:531-554).

This raises the issue of community crime control strategies aimed at prevention, in particular the dominance of policy preoccupations around the 'fear of crime', which has spawned an interest in tackling incivilities or anti-social behaviour. In reality this only creates the impression that the state is in control of crime, if it is compared with 'broken window' theory as it has been implemented in practice through so-called zero tolerance strategies of crime control. However, debates concerning the effectiveness of these policies are only seen as having only increased exclusion and the renewal of the death penalty, especially in the US (Ibid.).

The difficult with the death penalty is that it faces society with two dilemmas. To convict a person in a court of law there is a need to assess the offender's role and responsibility, and that is never going to be an easy task. In any investigation someone has to gather evidence effectively to be able to recognise what is significant, and honestly to convince the court, but we should recall who writes the statement and who interprets the law. It often happens that there are many influences behind the crime of murder. If society cannot justify how far the defender is responsible for the murder, society cannot justify how the defender should be punished, even before the trial.

As in most cases, it depends on the evidence or statement the prosecutor has submitted to the court of law and also on that recorded by the police. In some cases this can depend on the personality of the individual police officer and the honesty or sincerity of his or her recorded statement. It is often under these circumstances that corruption and miscarriages of justice occur in the process of justice. In most cases the victims of this are working-class people in Western countries or poor suspects in developing countries, who are financially disadvantaged and cannot afford to pay for a senior and experienced lawyer to represent them.

So far there are indicators of proposals in African countries to set up legal aid bureaus in all districts to advise the disadvantaged who have limited access to lawyers. For example, a declaration in the Malawi advocates a legal aid programme to provide legal assistance at all stages of the criminal process, including investigation, arrest, pre-trial detention, bail hearings, trials and appeals and any other proceedings.

Of course, experienced lawyers are not often available under legal aid, and the inexperienced lawyers provided by the state in Western countries to defend poor suspects are likely to lose the case to more experienced lawyers with influence within judicial circles. A rich suspect who can afford an expensive and experienced lawyer gets away with his or her crime, while the poor are the ones who are often found guilty and sentenced to barbaric capital punishment, even in certain circumstances being killed for a crime they did not commit. To make matters worse, for poor suspects in poor countries where is no provision for legal defence, in most cases their defence relies on the mercy and moral responsibility of the judge, who assesses the evidence provided by the prosecutor to reach his or her conclusion.

In the past independent observers have expressed concerns about the judicial system and the judicial focus on revenge due to political influence from either politicians, public reaction or misleading interpretations by the media of the purpose of justice and reconciliation. Especially in poor countries with undemocratic judicial systems controlled by the state, a judicial judgment depends on who is in power. Political judgments affect the impartiality of judges and sentencing tends to follow political policy and have a profound effect on people's lives.

This is again a violation of the Convention on Human Rights article 10. Trials are supposed to be impartial and without any prejudice. Corruption of judges and interference from the state or the media undermine the justice system. For instance, in the case of coloured suspects tried over the murder of a white middle-class person, the media, prosecutor, the judge and the jury may all be white and middle class, with little experience of what goes on in working-class areas and more especially how young people's background crosses over racial barriers at times.

Suspects in murder cases may even be tried and sentenced by the media or the majority public view before the trial takes place in court. In the same way, how do you justify that a trial is impartial when, for example, a white suspect is accused of being a mercenary in a black country and is tried by the local judiciary and media, who represents local people's interests. There are doubts about the justice system in any society where justice is practised by one racial group over another.

It is difficult to imagine how partiality and fairness can ever be achievable in countries where political influence is clearly allowed on the grounds of copying Western democratic systems, since Western countries' judges are appointed by the ruling party often on the grounds of being supporters or sympathisers of the ruling party. Under these political arrangements trials take place with officials who share the same values and political beliefs and ensure that a criminal who is perceived as being dangerous is dealt with in a manner that they perceive to be proper. In such a political or racial culture, the political system makes sure that no substantial evidence is ever presented in defence and where evidence is provided, it may be too insignificant and at best misleading.

However, two other points also need consideration. The first concerns the human rights position of an individual with regard to death penalty. Secondly, there is a need to look at whether violence may also be both rational and just in duly authorised, impartial and controlled law enforcement, in restraint of unlawful violence in a form of restraint of the insane. There is a degree of acceptance that those proved guilty should be disciplined or punished in a more humane way. On the other hand, the deliberate infliction of death on someone only gives the impression that the society believes in pain and death as morally justifiable treatment in a form of vengeance. That is a fundamental denial of the human rights of existence of fellow human beings, and in doing so society is returning evil for evil. The approach to the way society punishes murder, whether accidental, premeditated or an act of war, has to be holistic and corrective.

The emphasis of society must not be on killing offenders but on restoring their functional ability as responsible members of society. Restoration requires much more than punishment alone, it requires the offender to go beyond the pain and humiliation of the sentence to a fuller understanding of the consequences of his or her actions, why they are wrong and why something must be done about it. Otherwise, the passion of violence must be restrained by the loss of freedom until the person can be rehabilitated as a process of restoring them to be a responsible member of society. Nevertheless, this does not give the state the freedom to kill those who might not be guilty, nor to punish the guilty in excess. Even more important is that judges are not there just to punish, but essentially to protect the rights of individuals and, when it does become necessary to punish, to assess responsibility and to see that the punishment is not excessive.

Key aspects of punishment are that it should be allowed to foster links to treatment and rehabilitation. Where suspects are found guilty but new evidence subsequently raises doubt about this, the system must always provide room for a retrial, if there is valid evidence to warrant a judicial review. Therefore, society needs to reconsider the use of death penalty, as it deprives victims of the possibility of a second chance at trial. Despite that, some people argue that people deny themselves some of their rights when they commit a crime. If this type of indefensible argument is allowed it may lead to a number of miscarriages of justice, in that it is difficult, once again, to assess the truth, and moreover it is completely wrong to kill in the name of punishment. The use of punishment loses its meaning because no one knows whether to die is punishment until one has been there to tell the difference. A person is no less human because he or she has committed a crime.

Emerging evidence from deprived areas and countries recovering from war indicate a syndrome under which most people are traumatised by war and driven semi-mad, so that they cannot be judged on their actions alone but on a number of medical considerations. The death penalty should not be allowed as a kind of tribulation or vengeance, as it cannot repair the damage done to the victim or to the perpetrator. Justice, on the other hand, seeks to replace subjective anger with the desire to restore peace and equilibrium, so that society can continue to function healthily and for the good of all. Those who disagree with the use of the death penalty argue about how to get rid of the illusion that the death penalty is above all a means of reducing crime, and that in this role, according to social reformers, it is unthinkable. It is arguable that given that the role of institutions of correction such as detention centres, religious and educational institutions, and probation officers, doctors and psychologists, the rational choice is to emphasise behaviour change and rehabilitation. The idea of climate influencing behaviour dates back at least to the ancient Greeks and Romans (Bell et al., 1990). Therefore, broader theoretical perspectives on behaviour change should emphasise reconciliation.

Clearly, the continual institutional influence on changing criminal behaviour has been noted by most modern psychological theorists, who acknowledge to a greater or lesser extent that behaviour is variable and shaped by the context in which it occurs. Situations can also provoke crimes by engendering adverse emotional arousal, and dispositional theories argue that people have the motivation to commit crimes, but that the alternative solution to violent prevention is to fundamentally alter the political policies, attitudes and values of those who offend (Cornish, D. B., and Clarke, R. V., 1987: 933). Thus, considering the political element in most situations, and based on psychological theoretical perspectives, taking away another person's life is fundamentally an abuse of human rights. Nevertheless, the rational argument for the idea of the death penalty is that it reduces the burden on government expenses and is an alternative to keeping offenders locked up in prison. Various authors describe prison life, emphasising the division between prisoners and guards and the formation within the prison walls of two separate societies, each demanding adherence from its members to informal social rules and expectations (Clemmer 1958; Goffman 1961; Sykes 1958).

However, there are sound theoretical defences against such abuse of power. For instance, Michael Foucault argued that power should not be used to dominate others, but to provide knowledge; power invests in people and there is no power without awareness (Foucault, M. (1980), pp. 17–23). He saw power as a positively constitutive force. In this case since knowledge constitutes reality, if all forms of knowledge are also forms of power, then the reality is that power is a negative constraining force depending on who possesses the power. Thus, it can be argued that the use of the death penalty is a power that severely restricts the expiation of obtaining redress, towards the pursuit of individuals or the attribution of collective responsibility (Thomas, D. A., (1967), pp. 455–503). If the aim of the legal system is to transmit these values, the justice mechanism must also assist people to reconcile, rather than putting more weight on suffering and the death penalty. Criticisms of the death penalty from local human rights groups have expressed objections to the use of harsh treatment that contradicts the meaning of punishment. Human rights reports have highlighted people struck by fear caused by public executions, which have made many nervous about their treatment.

From the restorative aspect, there are arguments for a need to invest in a more satisfactory range of community-based forms of punishment, rehabilitation and reintegration into society in order to restore human relationships. Where such provision is compatible with the safety of the public, it seems to have a number of industrial advantages over the death penalty. One has only to point out some of the precautions to realise that capital punishment remains, even today, a spectacle that must be forbidden (Foucault, M. (1977), p. 15). I wish also to argue that in controlled punishment there is an element of denunciation and dealing with offenders, which is another way of making it clear to the perpetrators that their actions are not acceptable, rather than simply taking away their life.

On the other hand, this sort of restorative punishment must not be confused with locking prisoners up just to keep them away from the public, neither does it suggest keeping offenders in prison with treatment of a softly softly approach. Rather, it means a concerted effort to mould their behaviour by creating in their minds the ability to see something creative in themselves and the positive role they can play in that society to which they belong.

It is arguable that rehabilitation should involve various departments in assessing and diagnosing the problem. Those involved will soon discover that the actions of offenders are related to a number of issues, some of which are to do with themselves having been abused, others mental suffering, others a long-developed anger against social injustice that has developed into hatred of themselves and the injustice society has placed on them. It is as important to argue about the need for justice in times of injustice and conflict, and equally to bear in mind that the power of evil can easily become a culture within social structures, institutions and organisations. Such evil systems take years to develop and an equally long time to break down.

This is why restorative punishment has to make links with various institutions to foster rehabilitation. Treatment requires the spiritual prison chaplaincy, education, medicine, psychologists, social workers and probation to focus on different issues and ways to change. Education offers theoretical and practical skills and knowledge, and those required are increasingly trans-disciplinary and diverse. These skills need to be reflected in the societal infrastructure, either in training to improve someone's reasoning for better communication or especially in skills for less privileged individuals. This is associated with the use of analytical skills, cross-referencing, imaginative reconstruction and independent thinking. Offenders should be regarded as people in need of treatment rather than killing them. Evidence from human behaviour studies, especially in poor societies, proposes that the majority of offenders suffer from a mental disability and should be supported by a society that expresses a high regard for human life.

In conclusion, the idea of prison and detention centres once the suspect is convicted rather than the death penalty should be seriously considered by society at large and supported by all the countries in the world. This method also caters for another element in dealing with criminal offenders, which is the protection of society against the possibility of any harm that may be caused by these criminals.

The detention of offenders has the dual purpose of protecting the public as well as helping the perpetrators of crime. Not resorting to the elimination of such people will provide them with a second chance to go to court should fresh evidence emerge or to reform and start life afresh. Finally, I wish to reiterate the argument that whatever method of deterrence is used and however many criminals are killed, the element of crime will always remain in society. The only civilised response is to find a humane solution.

This is arguably related to development politics that are currently playing with new forms of violence and the consequent breakdown of militant political beliefs, which are posing a major question that begs an international response. There are at least four possible responses. The first is to do nothing and the second is to deny that anything needs to be done. The third response is more complex, because it requires a change in the world's powerful nations' minds to respond to the grievances that will have to include universal principles. The last is for Western countries to struggle together with developing nations to defeat poverty by opening up the market to establish a fair development structure, as it is applied in Western countries, so that developing countries can create local industries and commercial enterprises and seek to recover the skills of the long-term unemployed that are needed for development.

The recurrence of similar incidents in different areas is hard evidence of the argument that a society can strive to create a just society but can achieve the perfection of its own citizens in this matter. Returning to a theological explanation, society needs to continue helping its members to reform despite murderous acts. Society must not use violence to pretend that it is using discipline. If the death penalty is regarded as punishment it loses the meaning of discipline; instead, society must uphold the sanctity of human life and value the treatment of offenders as human beings. Therefore the emphasis in dealing with crime must work out how to change behaviour and should move from ideas of death penalty to those of treatment. Agents of society need to educate the public mind to this effect.

First and foremost, the success of the rehabilitation process in prison lies in creating an atmosphere of mutual trust, with expectations of responsible behaviour. Secondly, the provision of strong moral principles will enable and support changes in behaviour. Thirdly, the priority given to the relationship in prison and detention centres, notably the involvement of staff members who exemplify caring in the long term, may bear fruit in individuals committing themselves to accepted societal standards of behaviour towards each other.

Again, if the purpose of justice is to be served, offenders must be put in places where a change in behaviour and the realisation of their actions is seen as the best option and a remedy for their former damage by society itself. Rather than condemning them to be killed, this is restoring justice through a good relationship and healing them to reengage once again in a creative way in society. The process of reform is a question of balance. It is therefore imperative that a more responsible and civilised way is found in this generation to help offenders than merely condemning them to death.

I have looked at both sides of those suspected and found guilty of murder to show that it is hard to justify killing another life as punishment. Although it is in most people's interests that violent murderers should be removed from society to pay the price to their victims for the pain and the loss that relatives undergo, it is at the same time important that innocent suspects are protected from wrongful killing. Most of all, the presumption of innocence demands that the suspects' interests should be paramount.

Chapter eight

Conclusion

This book has considered the role of economic diversity in helping developing countries. The changing conditions of globalisation go beyond the concept of biological genetic theories of black underachievement that are championed by far right-wing scholars in their superiority theories. The assessment of wider violence in society has tried to show whether the measures that are currently in place are significantly reducing the extent of the problem of violence. It is quite clear that there is no shortage of agents of law and order, but on the other hand it is argued that the use of the law alone is a partial remedy for wider social breakdown in society and that the order that only society can create and maintain for itself has to come from within that society.

Therefore, the remedy always has to be the provision of resources to prevent a great division between those who have and those who have not. In a climate of insecurity, the threat of tomorrow is related to the question of public reaction to the tragic loss of life perpetrated by the criminal justice system. It is argued that it is a hard task to restore order in this situation, especially when there are groups with social grievances which do not only affect one generation but generations to come; in this kind of atmosphere human groups are filled with a rage for vengeance. This often produces a climate of fanatic militarism, which leads to conflicting interests together with the desire to place the protection of the public at the top of the law-and-order agenda. The concerns over and fear of fanatic militarism is real, genuine and valid, especially in the matter of fairness and justice and the inclusion of many others who have not engaged in violence as a matter of principle.

The book has argued that the lack of economic market equality and the universal treatment of all countries is the source of continual political conflicts. Hypotheses alone do not explain all conflicts, but they do identify factors likely to predispose groups to conflict. The book advocates a diversifying economic theory of the changing conditions of the twenty-first century that will reduce large horizontal inequalities. This is essential to eliminate a major source of conflict, since the increase of violence is conceived as not just a result of internal problems. World leaders need to pay particular attention to the social changes that will inevitably occur in adapting diversifying policies to slow down the political and economic deterioration.

Critical thinking skills are necessary to expose the wider and deeper implications underlying an unsustainable industrial society and the economic and ideological dominant influences playing an active role in developing countries' political decisions. Many Third World citizens wonder why Western countries have for so long ignored the foreign policies that create conflict in every developing country. And yet there is no evidence or hypothesis that solely explains the causes, apart from foreign ideological policies identified as factors likely to predispose groups to conflict.

The culture of violence allowed colonisers to diversify their dominance through forced labour or interference in the system of the ruling culture. Colonialism enabled them to provide cheap raw materials as well as a lasting trade market for the industrial countries. This is a combination of several factors of interdependence and inequality, organised in such a way that the benefits flows to the Western countries of the 'centre' and the disadvantages are meted out to the historically backward and underdeveloped ones on the periphery (Cfr. htt://www.landreform. org/Boff2.htm.). The export of raw materials with no value added has confined Africa to the Third World bracket, as well as subjecting it to dependence on development policies (Ibid.). Undue favour is shown to some countries and undue suspicion to others. Those from developed societies are favoured and get the best opportunities; those in poor countries sink down the social slippery slope. So the focus has to be on influencing developed countries' governments and practitioners. Third World countries need to launch a campaign website aimed at encouraging diversity in global developmental policies and engaging other civil society organisations in the cause.

For many years developing countries have, for instance, exported coffee. A company such as Nestlé buys the coffee beans for $1 a kilogramme, and roasts and grinds them to earn $20 per kilogramme, , which means that for each kilo sold Nestlé gains $19 profit (Cfr. htt://www.landreform.org/Boff2.htm.). Poor countries do not only lose money but also lose jobs. Take another example: cotton, whereby exports of the semi-processed lint cotton in effect cost poor countries several levels of jobs. There has been a great haemorrhage from the Third World economies. This also explains partly why poor countries cannot raise themselves from poverty. For instance, the 2006 talks in Geneva failed to reach an agreement for rich countries to reduce farming subsidies and lower import taxes. Oxfam charged the European Union with 'delaying tactics', which threatened to spoil the round of talks (Cfr. http://en.wikipedia.org/wiki/Doha-round). Millions of Africa's poorest farmers in remote areas shackled by unfair trade rules continues daily to be disenfranchised because of the colour of their skin.

Of course, the idea of development is not an isolated issue but one among many other theories. For instance, there are theories that mainly use a development theory to maintain the argument that the essence of the problem for poor countries is that their citizens lack the will to be modern. These theories argue that people do not embrace the idea of progress, and that they lack the kind of initiative that made the wealthy nations powerful. In addition, they conclude that because these countries are not competitive within the modern world economy and political order, their fate is clear: they were destined to supply the industrial world with agricultural and mineral resources (Nash, 1967:11-15). To be fair, it is important to look at both sides of the argument because it is easy to paint passive and unrepresentative views on both sides, so that one wonders what qualifies some countries to have such power over others forever.

In the view of local people, during colonial days choice was denied to them and regarded as irrelevant by the colonisers. Another statistic that should be shouted from the rooftops is that almost two-thirds of all children in Third World countries live in poverty. Two-thirds of the income of the worst-off countries goes in debt repayments and these are grievances that call for redress. Chronic poverty combined with financial insecurity is only one of the facts that countries living in debt have to face daily.

This state of economic dependence also stigmatises Third World countries, caught in a spiral of indebtedness, depressed and demoralised. Politicians and leaders are seen as just feeding their own stomachs and protecting their own interests, while ordinary citizens are left on their own to struggle for survival and millions live under stress. In addition, they faced an increased risk of teenage pregnancy, under-achievement at school, they lack motivation at work and do not look after themselves. These problems become worse in an economic downturn. One way forward is to offer more loans from the IMF or the World Bank, but a broader diversified legal definition is required of the commitment of globalisation to the improvement of poor countries. Not just individuals but also family businesses, religious groups and co-operative networks could join in.

Economic analysis estimates that diversity theory will play a pivotal role in helping developing countries gain at least stability, as well as meeting economic stimulus plans and win over critical politicians. The key argument is that societies are open for investors when all citizens globally operate with minimum constraints, which is vital to stimulate and revitalise the economy and to extend an olive branch to developing countries for political stability, rather than endlessly giving grants and loans that do little to help boost the economy, as the money is simply misused by dictators to keep them in power for ever.

Developing companies require an open economy and equality, as well as support for legislative change working within detailed legislative proposals. Given the current consultation about creating employment and improving public social services such as education, health, transport and housing in retirement, I feel that the time is right for the developed nations to explore the potential for diversifying policies to develop a model of trade tax tariffs, which reflect multiple interests and strengthen the ability and efficiency of poor countries to save for development of their national infrastructure and allow national governments to acquire a source of low-cost loans.

Developing countries, while often rich in resources, become dependent on foreign capital and expertise and lose their resources to foreign owners. This includes environmental damage wrought by transactional enterprises and fluctuating prices caused by external and global forces, which further diminish the well-being of peoples for whom survival itself is a struggle. Another assumption that needs to be mentioned is that poverty is the consequence of people being lazy, lacking in motivation and reluctant to accept change. This is an oversimplification of past influences and a failure to understand the rationale for the lack of economic development in poor countries and harm reduction in terms of the dominance of economic control strategies (Cfr. Innes, M. (2003). Understanding social control: deviance, crime and social order, Berkshire, Open University Press, chapter 5). The people are poor because they do not have industries; there is no employment because in the first place poor countries were meant to supply raw materials for industries elsewhere. This is an important theory related to the development idea, particularly concerning the endemic poverty of a severe system of economy that offers explanations for the culture of dependence on foreign aid.

It is quite simple to understand Eberhard Reuse's concerns about development aid. His analysis of Third World development policies is remarkably frank in its coverage and easy to understand. Reuse's thirty years of experience working with the international aid community lends significant credibility to the analysis he presents of the problems in the developmental aid paradigm and their potential solutions. Reuse presents a "practitioner's introduction" to developmental aid programmes followed by a thorough review of two programmes in Africa, giving details of the failures common to aid programmes through two case studies. Reuse's message of honesty, quality research and accurate self-evaluation are critical assets for any public servant. The ills of aid as described by the author (trends toward misjudgement, waste, inertia, complacency and arrogance) may permeate more than foreign aid programmes (Reusse, Eberhard. The Ills of Aid: An Analysis of Third World Development Policies. Chicago, IL: University of Chicago Press, 2002).

Nevertheless, worst of all are foreign policies that support dictators and keep them in power. It is unbelievable to see how dictators transfer wealth from the poorest countries to banks in the richest countries. Such political leadership simply subjects populations to poverty, further exploitation and a state of dependence on handouts with all this negativity.

While people recognise the benefit of foreign aid, on the other hand a wicked conspiracy has long kept the beautiful and virgin continent of Africa on its knees, impoverished its people and turned them into beggars, cry babies and laughing stocks of the global community (Reusse, Eberhard. The Ills of Aid: An Analysis of Third World Development Policies. Chicago, IL: University of Chicago Press, 2002.). For instance, what developmentally deprived communities need is aid with consultation over how the donated aid can empower the poor to participate in the process of self-reliance. Therefore, it is important for the leadership to explain to the poor how society cooperates in the social economy, and to realise that poverty does not just fall on some people by bad luck but through human agency, especially specific systems of interaction whereby the stakes are loaded against some and in favour of others.

However, what it is clear is that nature does not produce on one side owners of wealth and commodities, and on the other those born to be poor and possess nothing. It is argued that historical development is the product of developmental revolutions, of changes in a whole series of historical forms of social production. Some interests are unorganised; some rely on others to protect them; some are poorly organised. Society is dominated by those in power, wealthy and educated. Simmel uses the analogy of an organism and forcefully argues about its 'life force' - its power to resist, its healing power, and its ability to preserve itself - but he insists that these powers do not exist independently of the individuals in society but are the expression of their interaction (Simmel quoted by Craib, 1997:148-9).

Therefore, the concluding argument is that Western countries need to change their mind away from biological differences and examine the source of all that has happened the last 300 years, which may require a form of systems thinking that goes beyond a focus on the interaction of economic systems and requires the development of a world diversity system approach, which includes the interaction model of citizenship culture, politics and other human systems, reflects multiple identities and allegiances and strengthens the ability of each country to accommodate all races and to hold together. This is the only viable way and process of trying to find common ground in the quest for stability. The rational choice perspective of peace leaders must consider the implication of foreign policies, which is not simply making value judgments but is a relativist position that isolates developing countries from development and detracts them from concentrating on what matters to engage in conflicts.

In fact, this not only an irrational choice for development, as many scholars have used misleading arguments because they do not embrace developmental changes in developing countries as another way of discounting claims attributed to the lack of development. People from developing countries have yearned for so long for positive change, not necessarily a change of political guard but policies to tackle poverty and to end the use of violence, which would reduce conflicts and civil wars as well as being a positive developmental objective.

Thus, the mixture of foreign ideological policies and local poor leadership has prevented any significant change and as a result of poverty, deprived communities resort to the use of armed struggle to liberate themselves. The developing countries seek to benefit themselves by these conflicts through the sale of arms and controlling the making of decisions and choices. Though it is often unclear what the influence of arms dealers over foreign policies really is, there is significant influence on the economic level of aid in trade deals and it is under these ambiguous relations where the problem of conflicting interests in economic roles has been submerged within wider economic interests, which may be argued as having increased the fear of dominance to escalate the wider conflict.

For example, radical political groups denied a functioning role under the rule of a dictator and young people frustrated with unemployment view the Western political and economical system as eliciting discriminative stimuli, and therefore argue in favour of violent actions without the alternative of any contemplative deliberation. It is furthermore argued that the term radicalism or militarism has been assessed as describing the proposed role of foreign policies in developing countries' political conflict. Despite the fact that fanatics and fundamentalists have always existed, changes in society seem to have partly contributing to increasing beliefs in radicalism, a phenomenon that has been analysed to show a significant and steady influence on young people, especially in deprived areas. The reasons for the increase of violence in a wider context stem from a variety of factors, such as globalisation, information, religious drive, social and economic changes and long-term foreign ideological theoretical perspectives. This suggests a need for theories of developmental diversity in an equilibrium society where all nations are creatively allowed to live diversely; and to diversify policies in both developed and developing countries to put in place a foundation of stability and development.

From a conceptual level of foreign influence, the West must adopt a diversity policy of non-violence and end the glorification of the use of weapons, instead investing in research projects for peace in developing countries to reduce poverty, war-prevention strategic centres or missions that would respond immediately to prevent any further conflict occurring. Engaging the international community in regional disputes at an early stage, before they boil over into intensive political conflict, would east tensions, and at the same the international community can work together with the local population to promote diversity and cooperation. Unemployed skilled people in the West and millions of unemployed local citizens could engage in global projects, either in food production or in demonstrating peaceful living where all races live side by side with each other. From the perspective of multi-society cooperation, diversity situational variables are argued as having advantages for both investors and the host countries, serving needs that are beneficial within a wider contextual model.

What is implicit here is a need for a general standard of leadership that restricts dictatorship. World leaders, especially from industrial Western countries and the United Nations, need to draft a law and pass it as a leadership code of conduct or universal law that prohibits leaders from exceeding a certain agreed period in power. Any who disobey must be prosecuted and their political immunity removed by international law before their forceful removal. The United Nations must order a general referendum voting out such leaders and set up a new electoral commission and observers from the international community.

In most cases dictators appoint electoral commissions that serve to keep the dictatorship in power. If the leader is rejected in the referendum, he or she must step down with immediate effect and failure to so must lead to the country being isolated by the international community. All countries must operate under this law and impose an embargo on such a leader if he or she hangs on to power by the use of military rule. The developing strategy will only be achievable after democratic leadership is put in place. Development can only take place where all citizens are given a chance to vote and can entirely depend on transparency and accountability in a closer relationships between all nations and democratically elected political parties to meet the challenges ahead and to focus on making these countries self-sustaining and to utilise the resources at their disposal to propel them forward.

What is also important of course is for industrial countries to cease their heavy-handed control of the global trade market to allow all developing countries to compete fairly on the world market. One way to facilitate this is to embrace new technologies that add value to developing countries' products.

In areas that are in jeopardy from disorder there will have to be patience in the political system, a positive attitude and investment by the governing system in training the population for skills. Rather than investing in weaponry, developing human capacity allows a society to grow into an unknown future. The world is being shaken by the financial crisis, the credit squeeze and spiralling unemployment, which must nevertheless provide citizens with all kinds of creative opportunities. Mostly what developing society requires is experience and sensitivity where people can engage with these issues to adapt and repackage their resources. A logical step would be an exploration of the kind of society we want to live in. What about relationships and what about justice, and what does it look like in this society and this community?

Reinforcing the argument for sufficient stability challenges the population to embrace global technology, especially the use of electronic innovations in the agricultural sector, a major backbone of the economy, to double output through applying modern farming practices. According to experts, booming economies around the globe offer savvy investors an exciting world of opportunity. Like the market itself, sectors will experience periods of sustained growth, followed by periods of declining value due to a variety of factors and trends. In today's fast-paced global economy, there is a wide variety of investment vehicles to suit the individual needs of each investor (CNN.com/worldbusiness/23/01/09).

Finally, the lack of sensible economic development highlights a number of issues that have not yet been talked about in the current state of political and economic crisis, which still need to be considered before anything else. For example, land needs to be utilised productively, especially through organised settlements such as community villages, which among other things eases the process of delivering services such as health, clean water, communication and other social amenities to the people. It also calls for people to get more involved in the 2009 Performance Contracts, saying that they are not the sole concern of leaders. It is often pointed out that if development was to take root, each developing country should have an individual performance contract to supplement what their leaders have in place. People in developing countries need to adopt a saving culture to prepare for the future by utilising the banks and savings cooperatives, and to cultivate a spirit of unity and the habit of pooling resources as a source of strength, because individualism does not provide a channel to success.

The vision of creating opportunities for all to share development across the globe has been a crucial element of the grievances of the last few decades, arguing for a new society that works across global circles and highlighting a globalised scheme, developed within a wider perspective to readdress the mistakes created since the slave trade, when one race dominated an entire global population for their own benefit. The appropriate level of trust and support needed to foster diversity requires developed countries to be flexible. When all countries are open to sharing skills and knowledge it will be a stepping stone for addressing past problems. Globalisation together with development would increase stability and peaceful living together in society, rather than promoting a violent culture and criminal behaviours as a result of bad policies and selfish ideologies. Equality of condition means equality of opportunity; the same economic policies applied globally guarantee equality of treatment rather than emphasising differences.

Bibliography

Aguilar, M. I., (1996). The Rwanda Genocide and the Call to Deepen Christianity in Africa, Uganda: AMECEA GABA Publications Spearhead Nos. 148 – 150.

Allen, R. and Borror, G., (1982). Worship: Rediscovering the Missing Jewel. Pórtland: Multnomah Press.

Amelia, French, "Militias Raid Camps as New Offensive starts in the Killing Fields," The Independent, 16 December 1997.

Amnesty International Rwanda, "Arming the Perpetrators of the Genocide", London: Amnesty International Report, Index: AFR47/17/94 and (June 1995).

Anglican and Society, Report on World Conference of Churches, Geneva, WCC, September 1997

Anglican Communion, News Service, 21 March 1997.

Banks, R., (1994). Reconciliation and Hope, London: Paternoster Press.

Barham, E. L., (1961). Ruanda, a Bird's Eye View, London: Ruanda Mission CMS.

Barnett, Michael N., (2002). Eyewitness to a Genocide: The United Nations and Developing society. Ithaca, N.Y.: Cornell University Press.

Barrett, D. B., (1968). Schism and Renewal in Africa, Oxford: University Press.

Barrette, M. & McIntosh, M., (1980). "The Family Wage: Some Problems for Socialists and Feminists", 11 Capital and Class 51.

Battle, M., (1977). Reconciliation: The Ubuntu Theology of Desmond Tutu, Cleveland: The Pilgrim Press.

Baum, G., and Wells, H., (Ed.). (1997). The Reconciliation of Peoples, Challenge to the Churches, Geneva: WCC.

Bauman, Z., (1992). Intimation of Post Modernity, London: (Routledge & Kegan Paul).

Bayingana, Ng. E., (1994). "Reconciliation: Foundation for Reconstructing a New Rwanda", Nairobi: Evangel Press.

Beattie, J.O.C., (1968). Other Cultures, London: Hodder.

Beattie, Tina, (1994). Dominant Discourse and Silence Rebellions: Christianity, Culture and Liberation in the lives of African Women, Dissertation Presented to the University of Bristol towards a BA Degree.

Bennett, J., (1994). Zur Geschichte und Politik der Rwandischen Patriotischen Front, in: Schurings, H., (Ed). Ein Volk VerlaBt sein Land: Krieg und Volkermonrd in Ruanda, Koln: Neuer ISP Verl.

Berger Peter, (1966). Invitation to Sociology: London: Penguin.

Berger, P. L., & Luckmann, T., (1967). The Social Construction of Reality, Buckingham: Open University Press.

Berger, R., "Is Traditional Religion Still Relevant?" Orita, 3, (1969): 15-26.

Biggar, N., (1988). Theological Politics, Oxford: Latimer House.

Birinda, L., (1996). The Colour of Darkness: a Personal Story of Tragedy and Hope in Rwanda, London: Hodder and Stoughton Ltd.

Bournique, J., "Good Tidings", July – Oct. 1967, East Asia Institute Manila.

Bowen, R., (1995). Rwanda, Missionary Reflections on a Catastrophe, London: SPCK.

Bowen, R., (1996). Revivalism and Ethnic Conflict Questions from Rwanda, Transformation, Vol. 12, No. 2.

Braeckmann, Collète and A. Guillaume, La Poudrière Rwandaise, in Le Soir (Brussels), 1 J'une 1994

Brandstetter, Anna-Maria, (1997). "Ethnic or Socio-economic Conflict? Political Interpretations of the Rwandan Crisis", International Journal on Minority and Group Rights 4: 427 - 449, Institute for Ethnology and Africa Studies, Germany: Mainz University.

Branford, S., and Kucinski, B., (1989). The Debt Squads, London: Zed

Branson, Roy, "Never Again", Spectrum, Vol. 25, No. 4, June 1996

Briggs, S. M. & Chen, L.C., (Eds.), (1999). Humanitarian

Crises, The Medical and Public Health Response, London: Harvard University Press.

Brixton, British Council of Churches Report, Anglican and Racism 1986.

Brown, I. C., (1963). Understanding Other Cultures, Prentice Hall, Inc., Englewood Cliffs, New Jersey.

Burdon, C.R., (1964). "Theological Expository Times", February Issue.

Byrd, Anita, "Sabbath Slaughter: SDA's and Rwanda", Spectrum, Vol. 25, No. 4, June 1996.

Cassidy, M., (ed.), A Witness Forever, The Dawning of Democracy in South Africa, Stories Behind The Story, notes 1997.

Chopp, R., (1997). "Latin American Liberation Theology", in D. Ford (Ed.). The Modern Théologiens, Oxford: Blackwell.

Chrétien, J. P., (1991). Presse libre' et Propagande Raciste au Rwanda: Kangura et 'Les 10 Commandements du Hutu, Politique Africaine 42

Chrétien, Jean-Pierre, "Tournant Historique au Burundi et au Rwanda", in Marches tropicaux et méditerranées, Paris, Octobre 1993.

Classe, L. P., "Ils Trébuchaient dans les Ténèbres", Grands Lacs, no. Special, 1 March 1935.

Coleman, Alice, (1988). Design Disadvantage and Design Improvement; The Criminologist, vol. 12

Conn, H. M., (1984). Eternal Word and Changing Words, London: ECUM.

Cormack, D., (1989). Peacing Together, London: MARC Europe.

Cumberland Lodge, a Residential Conference Essay, "Minority Rights and Reconciliation in the Commonwealth", 11th – 13th February 2004

Dallaire, Roméo, A., (2004). Shake Hands with the Devil: The Failure of Humanity in Developing society. Toronto: Vintage Canada.

Dalton, G., (Ed.), (1967). Tribal & Peasant Economics, Readings in Economic Anthropology, Texas: Press Sourcebooks in Anthropology.

David Simon & Anders Narman (Eds), "Development as Theory and Practice", Harlow. Longmann,

Danzig, R. and Lowry, M., (1975). "Everyday Disputes and Mediation, Law and Society Review", Volume 9 Number 4, pages 675-694

de Waal, Alex, "The Genocidal State", in the Times Literary Supplement, London, 1 July 1994

Denzin, N. K., (1970). The Research Act in Sociology, Chicago: Aldine

Des Forges, Alison, (1999). "Leave None to Tell the Story", Genocide in Developing society. New York: Human Rights Watch.

Destexhe, Alain; Showcross, William, Translated by Marschner, (1996), Rwanda and Genocide in the Twentieth Century, New York: New York University Press.

Diamond, S., (1971). "The Rule of Law versus the Order of Custom" 38 Social Research 42

Dickson, K. A., (1984). Theology in Africa, London: Lutterworth

Diener, E., and Crandall, R., (1978), Ethics in Social and Behavioural Research, Chicago: University of Chicago Press.

Djereke, Jean Claude, (1995), "Peace and Reconciliation in Rwanda, What can the Church do"? Vidyajyoti Journal of Theological Reflection, Vol. 59, No 4, April.

Dorsey, L., (1994). Historical Dictionary of Rwanda, London: The Scarecrow Press.

Doyle, Mark, "Ex-Rwandan P.M. Reveals Genocide Planning", BBC News. 26 March 2004

Donoghune, Joan, "Freedom of Information Act release" by the Department of State, 16th May 1994

Duignan, P., (Ed.), (1971). Belgianism in Africa 1870-1960, Vol. 1: The History and Politics of Belgianism 1870-1914, London: SCM.

Duly, G., "Creating Violence – Free Society: The Case of Rwanda", Journal of Humanitarian Assistance, July 20, 2000.

Dussel, E., (1976). History and Theology of Liberation, New York: Orbis Books.

Erickson, J., (1996). The International Response to Conflict and Genocide: Lessons from Rwanda Experience, Odense: SCLEAR.

Evans-Pritchard, E. E., (1937). Witchcraft, Oracles and Magic Among the Azande, Oxford: Clarendon Press.

Evans-Pritchard, E. E., (1965).Theories of Primitive Religion. Oxford: Clarendon Press.

Farley, E., (1996). Deep Symbols: Their Post-modern Effacement, Minneapolis: Fortress Press.

Farmer, H. H., (1935). The World and God, London: Nisbet

Fieldhouse, D. K., (1961). "Imperialism; a Historiographical Revision"; Revision; Economic History Review, X1V, 2

Forde, D., (1954). "African Worlds", Oxford: Oxford University Press.

Franche, D., (1995). Généalogie du Génocide Rwandais: Hutu et Tutsi; Gaulois et Francs? Les Temps Modernes 582(50ᵉ année).

Frank, A. G., (1981). CRISIS: In the Third World, London: Heinemann.

Frankel, S. H., (1955). The Economic Impact on Underdeveloped Societies, Cambridge: Harvard University Press.

Frisby, D., (1984). George Simmel, Chichester: Ellis Harwood.

Frost, B., (1991). The Politics of Peace, London: Longman and Todd Ltd.

Gana, A. T., (1994). The African Political Crisis and the Church in Africa, London: SPCK

Gatwa, Tharcisse, (1995). "Revivalism and Ethnicity", The Church in Rwanda, Transformation, Vol. 12, No.2, April/June.

George, S., (1988). A Fate Worse than Debt, London: Penguin

George, S., (1992). Debt Boomerang: How Third Word Debt Harms Us All, London: Pluto

Gerloff, R., (1998). Truth, a new Society and Reconciliation: the Truth and Reconciliation Commission in South Africa a German Perspective, Leeds: University Press.

Gill, Robin, (1985). A Textbook of Christian Ethics, Edinburgh: T & T Clark.

Gillingham, Richard, "Quodlibet" Journal: Vol. 7, Number 2, April June 2005.

Gluckman, Max, "Seven Year Research Plan of the Rhodes – Livingstone Institute: Human Problems in British Central Africa": The Rhodes – Livingstone Journal, No. 4, December 1945.

Gluckman, Max, (1965). Politics Law and Ritual in Tribal Societies. Oxford: Blackwell.

Goldhor, L. H., (1990). The Dance of Anger. Wellingborough, Grapevine.

Goodhand, J. and D. Hulme, (1999). "From Wars to Complex Political Emergencies: Understanding Conflict and Peace Building in the New World Disorder", Third World Quarterly 20 (1).

Goose, S., and Smyth, D., (1994). "Arming Genocide in Rwanda" Foreign Affairs 73 (5)

Goulet, Denis, (1971). "International Journal of Social Economics", 2411 Development Ethics, a new discipline, University of Notre Dome, Indiana, USA.

Goulet, Denis, (1971). The Cruel Choice: A New Concept in the Theory of Development, Centre for the study of development and social change, New York: Atheneum.

Gourevitch, Philip, (1998). We Wish to Inform You That Tomorrow We Will Be Killed With Our Families: Stories from Rwanda, New York: Farrar Straus, and Giroux.

Government of Rwanda, "Capacity Needs Assessment and Capacity Building for Rwanda's Economic Management Institutions", Kigali June 2000.

Government of Rwanda, "Poverty Reduction Paper, Ministry of Finance and Planning Kigali", June 2002.

Gray, R., this is a paper originally submitted to the conference "on Changing Society", held in August 1977 to mark the quincentenary of Uppsala University.

Green, J. B, Mark, D., Baker, (2000). Recovering the Scandal of the Cross: Atonement in New Testament and Contemporary Contexts, London: Intervarsity Press.

Green, R., (1990). A Step Too Far, Exploration into Reconciliation, London: Longman and Todd.

Greene, L., (1988). The Power to the Powerless, Basingstoke: Marshall, Morgan and Scott.

Greham, S. J., (1965). Theology of St. John. London: Hodder

Guichaova, A., (1997). "Les Antécédents Politiques de la Crise Rwandaise de 1994", Arusha.

Gutierrez, Gustavo, "Praxis of Liberation and Christian Faith", (San Antonio 1974).

Gutierrez Gustavo, (1988). A Theology of Liberation History Politics and Salvation, London: SCM Press Ltd.

Harris, D., "The world's nations knowingly did nothing about the slaughter of one million Tutsi and moderate Hutu" in Church Times, Newspaper, 31st August 2001

Harris, E. H., (1968), A Ministry Renewed. London: SCM Press Ltd

Harris, Richard, (Ed.), (1975). The Political Economy of Africa, Cambridge, Mass: Schenkman.

Harvey, Cox, (1965). The Secular City, London: SCM Press.

Hastings, A., "The Tribal Contest behind Africa's Bloodbath" The Tablets, 5 September 1998.

Hebga, M., "Penance and Reconciliation in African Culture", African Ecclesial Review 25, 1983, pp. 347-355.

Hegba, M., article, "un Concile a I' Heure de I' Afrique" in 'Personnalité Africaine et Catholicisme', Paris, 1962

Hillman, E., (1975). Polygamy Reconsidered, African Plural Marriage and the Christian Churches, New York: Orbis Books.

Hinga, Teresa, (1994). "Jesus Christ and the Liberation of Women in Africa", in King (Ed.) Feminist Theology from the Third World, Maryknoll: Orbis Books.

Hirst, R. J., (1959). The Problems of Perception, London: Allen & Unwin.

Hort, A. F., (1896). Life and Letters of Fenton Anthony Hort, 1 & 2, London: Macmillan.

Hort, A. F., (1977). Just Men, London: Epworth Press.

Huband, Mark, "Church of the Holy Slaughter", the Observer, 5 June 1994

Hughes, A. J., (1963). East Africa: The Search for Unity, New York: Penguin Books.

Human Rights Watch, Report, UN Human Rights Commission of 11th November 1994

Hurley, M., (1974). "Reconciliation, in Religion and Society", Belfast: Institute of Irish Studies.

Ilongu, E., "Indigenization of Imported Religious", Journal of Asian and African Studies, XIV, 1-2, 121-128.

Kaldor, Mary, (2003). Global Civil Society, An Answer to War, Oxford: Blackwell Publishers Ltd.

Kalilombe, P., (1991). Black Catholics Speak, Reflection on Experience, Black Catholics Speak, Reflection on Experience, Faith Theology, London: Catholic Association for Racial Justice.

Kalilombe, P. A., (1979). "The Salvific Value of African Religions". Afer, 21, pp.143–157.

Kamukama, D., (1993). "Pride and Prejudice in ethnic relations, Rwanda", p.133-160, in: P. Anyango (Ed.) Arms and Daggers in the Heart of Africa: Studies on internal conflicts. Nairobi: Academy Science Publication.

Kant, E., (1934). The Critique of Pure Reason, trans. Meiklejohn, J. M. D. London: Dent.

Kimenyi, A., (1989). Kinyarwanda and Kirundi Names, The Edwin Millen Press.

Kirk, J. A., (1979). Liberation Theology, An Evangelical View from the Third World, England: Marshalls Theological Library

Kirk, J. A., (1980). Theology Encounters Revolution: Leicester

Knight, Frank, H. and Merriam, Thorton, (1947). The Economic Order and Religion, Kegan Paul Tench Trubner Co. Ltd.

Kofi, Annan, Fellowship, April 2001, Vol. 6, No.2.

Kolini, Emmanuel, (1995). "Towards Reconciliation in Rwanda", Transformation, Vol. 12, No2, April/June.

Kritzinger, J. J., (1996). The Rwandese Tragedy as Public Indictment of Christian Mission, London, SPCK.

Lakeland, P., (1997), Post Modernity: Christian Identity in a Fragmented Age, Minneapolis, Minn.: Fortress.

Lemarchad, Rene, (1970). Managing Transition Anarchies: Rwanda, Burundi, and South Africa in Comparative Perspective, London: Marshall Morgan & Scott.

Lemarchand, Rene, (1994). "Managing Transition Anarchies: Rwanda, Burundi, and South Africa in Comparative Perspective", the Journal of Modern African Studies, 32, 4, Cambridge: University Press.

Lenski, G., Nolan, P., and Lenski, J., (1995). Human Societies, an Introduction to Macro Sociology, Seventh Edition, New York: McGrawHill, Inc.,

Lerner, H. G., (1990). The Dance of Anger, Wellingborough: Grapevine.

Linden, Ian, (1977). Church and Revolution in Rwanda, Manchester: Manchester University Press.

Linden, Ian, (1997). "The Church and Genocide, Lessons from Rwandese Tragedy", in Baum, Gregory & Wells, Harold (Des). The Reconciliation of peoples, Challenges to the Churches, Maryknoll, NY: Obis Books; Geneva: WCC Publications, pp.41-43.

Loewen, Jacob, "Mythological and Mission". Practical Anthropology, Vol.16n. 4, July-August, 1969.

Longman, Timothy, (2006). "Justice at the Grassroots"? Gacaca Trials in Rwanda in Naomi Roht-Arriaza and Javier Mariezcurrena, (Ed). Transitional Justice in the Twenty-First Century, Beyond Truth versus Justice. Cambridge, New York: Cambridge University Press.

Luzbetak, L. J., (1963). The Church and Culture, an applied anthropology for the religious worker. Divine Word Publication Techny. Illinois USA

Maluleke, T. S., (1997). "Truth, National Unity and Reconciliation in South Africa, Aspects of the Emerging Theological Agenda", Missionalia, 25:1 April, pp.59-86.

Mamdani, Mahmood, (2001). When Victims Become Killers. Belgianism, Nativism, and the Genocide in Rwanda, Oxford: Currey.

Maquet, J.-J., (1954). Le Système des Relations Sociales dans le Rwanda Ancien. Tervuren: Musée, (Annales du Musée royale du Congo belge, Sciences de l'homme, ethnocide, 1).

Markowitz, M. D., (1973). Cross and Sword: the Political Role of Christianity Mission in the Belgian Congo, 1908-1960. Stanford.

Martey, E., (1993). African Theology, Inculturation and Liberation, New York: Orbis Books.

Maxwell, G. and Morris, A., (2001), "Putting Restorative Justice into Practice for Adult Offenders", Howard Journal of Criminal Justice, Vol. 40

Mbanda, L., (1997). Committed to Conflict, The Destruction of the Church in Rwanda, London: SPCK.

Mbiti, J. S., (1991). Concepts of God in Africa. London: S.P.C.K.

McCullum, Hugh, (1995). The Angels Have Left Us. The Rwanda Tragedy and the Churches, with a foreword by Desmond Tutu, Geneva: World Council of Churches.

McKinnley Jr., 'International Herald Tribute', 16 December 1997.

Minasse, H., (1961). United Nations Consideration of domestic questions and of their International Effects, Columbia University.

Molt, P., (1994a). Der Pyrrhussieg der 'Patritischen Front' in Ruanda, Konrad-Adenauer-Stiftung Auslandsinformationen/KAS-AI 5:3-38

Mudimbe, V.Y., (1994). The Idea of Africa, Bloomington and Indianapolis: Indiana University Press, London: James Curey.

Muzorewa, G. H., "African Liberation Theology", in Voices from the Third World, 31 January 1990, pp.190-97

Nash, M., (1967). In Tribal & Peasant Economies, Readings in Economic Anthropology Texas, Press Sourcebooks in Anthropology, London: University of Texas Press.

Neckbrouck, V. (1971). Afrique Noire et la Crise Religieuse de l' Occident'. T.M.P. Tabora, Tanzania: Book Department.

Newbigin, L., (1989). The Gospel in a Pluralistic Society, London: SPCK.

Newbury, M., C., (1988). The Cohesion of Oppression: Clientship and Ethnicity in Rwanda 1860 -1960. New York: Columbia University Press.

Newbury, D., (1998). "Understanding Genocide", ASR 41

Newbury, Catherine. and D. Newbury, (2000). "Bringing the Peasants Back, in Agrarian Themes in the Construction and Corrosion of Statistic Historiography in Rwanda", AHR105, 3.

Newbury, Catherine, (2002). Genocide, Collective Violence, and Popular Memory, the Politics of Remembrance in the Twentieth Century, Ethnicity and the Politics of History in Rwanda, New York: Schoerly Resources Inc.

Nguema, I., "the Challenges for Peace Making in Africa, Conflict Résolution, Addis–Ababa, Ethiopia", London: International Alert Report, September 1994

Nisbet, Robert, (1962). Community & Power, New York: Oxford University Press.

Nkundabagenzi, Article. "Les chefs du Rwanda expriment leur loyalisme envers le Mwami", Le Courrier d'Afrique (1 Octobre 1956), Rwanda Politique

Nothomb, D., (1965). Un Humanism Africain, Editions Lumen Vitae, Bruxelles.

O'Connell, J., "The Essence of the Forgiveness", Month CCLV (September/October 1995)

Okoth, P. G., (Ed.). (2000). Africa at the Beginning of 21st Century, Nairobi: University Press.

Oliver, R., & Fage, J. B., (1962). A Short History of Africa, London: Penguin African Library.

Onimode, B., (1987). The Political Economy of African Crisis. London: ZED.

Ordway, T., (1945). Democratic Administration, New York: Association Press.

Osborn, H. H., (1965). Revival – A Precious Heritage, Winchester: Apologia Publications.

Pabanel, J.P., (1995). Bilan de la deuxième République Rwandaise: du Modèle de développemental a la violence générale, Politique Africaine 57:112-123.

Parsons, T., (1951). The Social System, New York: Free Press.

Parsons, T., (1969). Politics and Social Structures, New York: The Free Press.

Perry, B., (2002). Hate Crime and Identity Politics, London: Thousands Oaks.

Pirouet, L., (1989). Christianity Worldwide, Church History 4: AD1800 Onwards, London: SPCK

Popper, K., (1945:1). The Open Society and its Enemies, London: Routledge and Keegan Paul.

Pottier, Gerard, (1995). The Rwandese Crisis 1959-1994, History of Genocide, London: C. Hurst & Co.

Présence Africaine, (1957). Rencontres: Des Prêtres noirs s'interrogent, Paris: 3me éd. Paris.

Prunier, G., (1995). The Rwanda Crisis: History of a genocide, New York: Columbia University Press

Randall, J., "News Post on Rwanda", Washington Post, 29 June 1994.

Reith, C., (1956). The Blind Eye of History, London: Oliver & Boyd.

Resistance "as a Form of Christian Witness", Geneva, WCC/CWME-URM, 1986

Reyntjens, Filipe, (1985), Pouvoir et doit an Rwanda, Tervuren, Musée Royal de l'Afrique Centrale, Paris.

Reyntjens, Filipe, "The Proof of the Pudding is in the Eating": in the Journal of Modern Africa Studies, Cambridge, 31, 4, December 1993, pp. 563-83

Reyntjens, Filipe, (1994a). L'Afrique des Grands lacs en Crise: Rwanda, Burundi, 1988–1994, Paris: Karthala.

Reyntjens, Filipe, (1995). Rwanda: Trois Jours Qui ont Fait Basculer L'histoire. Bruxelles, Paris: Institut africain -CEDAF/Afrika institut-ASDOC; L 'Harmattan.

Robinson, A. R. and Borror, G., (1982). Worship: Rediscovering the Missing Jewel, Portland: Mutnomah Press.

Robinson, J. A. T., (1965). The New Reformation, SCM Press.

Roosens, E., (1989). Creating Ethnicity: The process of Ethnogenesis, Newbury Park: Sage Publications.

Rosenthal, James, M. and Currie, Nicola, (1997) "Being Anglican", compiled by James M. Rosenthal and Nicola Currie, Anglican Consultative Council X, Panama City

Rubenstein, R. & Roth, J. K., (1987). Approaches to Auschwitz, the Legacy of the Holocaust, London: SCM Press Ltd.

Russell, B., (1968). The Autobiography of Bertrand Russell, 3 Voles, London: George

Russell, B., (2002). Research Methods in Anthropology: Qualitative and Quantitative Methods. Walmit Greek: Altamira Press.

Sanders, E. R., (1969). "The Hamitic Hypothesis: its Origin and functions in time Perspective", Journal of African History 10, 4: 521 – 532.

Sapir, Edward, (1949). Selected Writings of Edward Sapir in Language, Culture and Personality, David G. Mandelbaum, Ed. Berkeley, USA: University of California Press.

Scheer, Gray, (1995). "Rwanda, Where was the Church?" Evangelical Missions Quarterly, Vol. 31, No.3, July

Schreiter, R. J., (1992), Reconciliation, Mission & Ministry in Changing Social Order, New York: Orbis Books.

Sheppard, D., (1983). Bias to the Poor, London: Hodder and Stoughton.

Shorter, A., (1973). African Culture and the Christian Church, London: G., Chapman.

Shorter, A., (1975). Prayers in the Religious Traditions of Africa, Oxford University Press.

Shriver, D. W., "An Ethnic for Enemies: Forgiveness in Politics", Woodstock Report, Oxford: Oxford University Press, March 1996, No. 45

Smith, A. C. Stanley, (1946). Road to Revival. The Story of Ruanda Mission, Forwarded by Canon M.A.C. Warren, London: CMS.

Smith, J. C. and Hogan Brian, (1992). Criminal Law, Seventh Edition, London: Butterworths.

Southall. A., (1961). Social Change in Modern Africa, London: Oxford University Press.

Taylor, J. V., (1963). The Primal Vision, London: S.C.M

Tedaro, M. P., (1977). Economics for a Developing World, an Introduction to Principles, Problems and Policies for Development, London & New York: Longman.

Temple, William, (1934). Nature, Man and God, London: Macmillan.

Temple, William, (1976). Christianity and the Social Order, (Edition), London: SPCK.

The Church Times News, London: Church House, 5 September 1997, p.2

The Church Times News, London: Church House, 31 August 2001, p.4

The Historical Journal, xiiv, 2, (1969), pp. 285–301

The New Yorker, Magazine, New York: 26 May 1998.

Tillich, P., (1954). The Interpretation of History, New York: Scribner.

Tillich, P., (1959). Theology of Culture, New York, OUP

Tonkin, E., (1992). Narrating Our Pasts: The Social Construction of Oral History, Cambridge: University Press.

Trainer, T., (1989). Developed to Death, London: Green Print.

Tschury, T., (1997). Ethnic Conflict and Religion Challenge to the Churches, Geneva: WCC Publications.

Turner, Harold, W., (1969). "The Place of Independence Religious Movements in the Modernisation of Africa": Journal of Religion in Africa, 2, p.43-63.

Tutu, D., (1993). "African Theology and black Theology: The Quest for Authenticity and the Struggle for Liberation", in

African Challenge, edited by Kenneth Best, Nairobi: Trans Africa Publishers.

Tutu, D., (1997). Foreword, in BOTMAN & PETERSEN 1996a, 78

Tutu, Desmond, (1997). "Troubled but not Destroyed", Unpublished Presidential Address, All African Conference of Churches, Seventh General Assembly, Addis Ababa, October, 1997

UN Global Agenda, the human poverty indicator 2000.

UNHCR Representative Report, Kampala, Uganda, June 1984.

Uvin, P. and Warren, M. A. C., (1994). Aiding Violence: The Development Enterprise in Rwanda, London: Church Missionary Society.

Vold, G., Bernard, T., and Snipes, J., (2002). Theoretical Criminology, Oxford: Oxford University Press.

Volf, M., (1996). Exclusion and Embrace: A Theological Exploration of Identity, Otherness and Reconciliation, Nashville: Abingdon Press.

Vygotsky, L. S., (1978). Mind in Society: the Development of Higher Psychological Process, in M. Cole, V. John Steiner, S. Scribner, E. Souberman (Eds.). Cambridge, MA: Harvard University Press.

Waldmeir & Holmam, Financial Times, (London), 18 July 1994, p.1

Walsh, M., and Davies, B., (Ed.). (1984). Proclaiming Justice and Peace, Document from John xxiii to John Paul ii, London: Collins Liturgical Publications.

Watson, C., Issued paper, "Exile from Rwanda: Background to an Invasion". Washington: The U.S. committee for refugees, February 1991.

Welbourn, F. B., (1965). East African Christian, London: Oxford University Press.

Wiesel, Elie, Speech while receiving, Nobel Peace Price, 1986 Evangelical Missions Quarterly, Vol. 33, No. 4, October.

Woodward and Pattison, (2000). The Blackwell Reader in Pastoral and Practical Theology, Oxford: Blackwell Publishers Ltd.

Woodward, C. Vann, (1971). American Counterpoint, Slavery and Racism in the North South Dialogue, Boston: Little, Brown.

World Bank, "World Bank Debt Tables 1989/90 First Supplement 1989", Washington DC: World Bank.

Yoder, J. H., "Exodus and exile: the two faces of liberation", Missionalia, Pretoria: 2, 1, 1974.

Lectronic sources

http://www.sedos.org/english/liden2.htm/12/8/07
http://www.sedos.org/english/liden2.htm/12/8/07
http://news.yahoo.com/s/afp/20080215/
sc_afp/sudanfrancearchaeology_080215201642;_
ylt=AsVyfwTgpxINUkUEsRwE._xFeQoB
www.bbc.co.uk/history/ancient/bri19/8/2002